Exploring Shakespear

Romeo *and* Juliet

Approaches and activities

Susan Leach

Oxford University Press 1994

Oxford University Press, Walton Street, Oxford OX2 6DP

Oxford New York Toronto
Delhi Bombay Calcutta Madras Karachi
Kuala Lumpur Singapore Hong Kong Tokyo
Nairobi Dar es Salaam Cape Town
Melbourne Auckland Madrid

and associate companies in
Berlin Ibadan

Oxford is a trade mark of Oxford University Press

Introduction © Susan Leach 1994
Ways In, The Play and Overview © Susan Leach 1994

Published by Oxford University Press 1994

A CIP catalogue record for this book is available from the British Library

ISBN 0 19 831286 5

Printed in Great Britain at the University Press, Cambridge

Acknowledgements

The cover illustration is by Anthea Toorchen.

The handwriting is by Elitta Fell.

The publishers would like to thank the following for permission to reproduce
photographs:

Ancient Art and Architecture Collection pp. 31, 47, 59; Bridgeman Art Library Ltd.
p. 85 top right and middle; Donald Cooper Photostage pp. 52 left and middle, 54,
85 top left and bottom right; Explorer/Martel Olivier p. 48; Robbie Jack pp. 21, 30
both, 52 right, 85 bottom left; Kobal Collection p. 42.

Contents

Overview

Introduction

These student study books to accompany *Romeo and Juliet, A Midsummer Night's Dream,* and *Julius Caesar* are intended primarily for Year 9 students working towards KS3 of the National Curriculum in English.

As they all offer a wide range of activities they can also be used with other secondary students, particularly those in years 10 and 11 working towards GCSE English and English (Literature).

The general purpose of the books is to enable the inexperienced student, probably coming to Shakespeare for the first time, to make sense of the plays from the start, and to find enjoyment in reading and working on them. We also hope that students' self-confidence in tackling Shakespeare will grow as a result of using these books, and that they will go on with enthusiasm to read and enjoy other plays by Shakespeare.

Each of the three books mirrors the individuality of its author, as well as reflecting a common approach to the study of the plays, based on active, collaborative work. The differences between the three books also reflect the very different natures of the three plays; however common the approach, each play demands its own separate treatment.

The books follow a common format:
1   An Introduction to Active Approaches, aimed at the teacher, which provides a simple explanation of the active approaches used across all three books; and a Ways In section, which offers students ideas for introductory work on the plays, before full study is begun. For students who already know the basic plot and characters, some of these suggestions will be redundant.
2   Activities on the play itself, scene by scene.
3   An Overview section, which offers activities to help students look back at the plays and consider them as complete entities, from a variety of viewpoints related to themes, imagery, language, characters, and plot.

The second section, of scene-by-scene activities on the play, requires a little more clarification. It has been organized so that usually more than one activity is offered for each scene. It is assumed that teachers will not work through these activities from start to finish, but will select assignments from the range on offer.

Scenes are prefaced by a brief resumé of their importance to the play, with an indication of their time and place. *Exploring Shakespeare: Romeo and Juliet* makes most obvious reference to time, with fewer specific references in *A Midsummer Night's Dream*. *Julius Caesar* is concerned with only a few salient calendar dates, and assumes the passing of time without mentioning it, so this has few specific references.

Where an activity refers to specific lines of text within a scene, a line reference is given, based on the *Oxford School Shakespeare* edition of the play.

Activities which require a cleared space for students to work in are marked in the text with an icon ▨. These activities are often the most challenging for the teacher to organize and oversee, so they may not be the first choice of teachers who are still 'finding their Shakespeare feet'!

Scene-by-scene activities are based on approaches designed to fulfil several purposes:

- to enable students to engage with the underlying concerns of the plays
- to encourage students to think for themselves, and be prepared to offer their own ideas and conclusions
- to help students work independently of direct supervision by the teacher, alone, in pairs, and in groups
- to take students into a deeper knowledge and understanding of the plays than is implied by the narrow requirements of KS3 SATs.

The activities suggested throughout the scene-by-scene pages include acting, improvisation, mime, freeze frames, and other use of voice and movement; written, visual/illustrative and stage/theatrical assignments; discussion, hotseating, and inquests; and searching and researching. The emphasis throughout is on taking on the language of the plays as it stands – on using its differences and challenges positively and creatively.

We suggest that students have a journal, log, or notebook for the written activities, especially for those which ask them to note down their thoughts or reactions. (Sometimes the word 'journal' is used in the students' books.)

These books can be used in different ways to fit in with students' previous experience. Where students have already read the play, or seen a film version of the play, the activities will help them explore the play in greater depth, and with help, consolidate what they already know. Where students are coming to the play for the first time, it is possible to run the student study book alongside the reading of the play. The preferred approach will need to be thought through by the teacher. Each way of using these students' books will produce different results and reactions in the classroom.

Assignments in the scene-by-scene sections make clear how students should be grouped, and sometimes suggest that they should get their teacher to help them. It has been taken for granted that teachers will set up each lesson, but the emphasis is always on students doing these assignments for themselves. They are consistently addressed as 'you' in active collaboration with each other.

Introduction to active approaches

Many of the active approaches used in these books are already well-established as good classroom practice, while others are based on techniques developed by theatre practitioners.

Reading

Because students coming new to Shakespeare are unfamiliar with Shakespeare's language and verse form, it is useful to have a range of reading techniques at hand to help them grasp the meaning of the texts. The reading techniques described below emphasize particular features of different kinds of text. All the techniques can be used with pairs, groups, or whole classes. They are designed to involve all students in reading. Success with these techniques depends on all students using the same edition of the play, because of variations in punctuation between editions.

It is advisable to try out all these reading techniques with a class, so that students know how to use them when working independently.

Reading by punctuation marks

Have students seated in a large circle if possible. They read in turns round the group, each person stopping and handing on to the next person at a punctuation mark.

Reading by punctuation marks makes long speeches in blank verse manageable for students, and helps them grasp the ideas and development of thought in a speech. The words between punctuation marks express one idea or thought, even the word 'and': every speech moves from an opening statement, question, or proposition to another position. The technique highlights single words and images, and helps students identify metaphor and imagery. Many assignments which ask students to find key words and images, thoughts and feelings in the text depend on this reading technique.

Where students are using this technique in a pair or a small group, the same method applies.

Reading by 'sense units' (usually marked off by full stops, semicolons or the word 'and') is a variation of this. It invites students to ignore commas and read on until there is a sense 'pause', rather than having maybe only a single word to read.

Reading by sentences

This technique allows whole thoughts to be read/heard at once. The irregularity of sentence length in speeches and the linking of thoughts are clearly shown by using this method. A development of this is to write out each sentence separately to see how the thinking has moved on from one idea to the next. Some assignments build on this by asking students to headline the main thought in a sentence.

Reading by speeches

Many scenes in the plays work best with one person reading the whole of any speech, and the next person reading the next speech, and so on round the group. This retains whole group involvement, without burdening individuals with the responsibility for 'parts'. It allows the cohesion of each character's words to be taken in, and is a good technique to use when whole scenes are being read in which no character speaks more than about six lines at once.

A mixture of all techniques can be used in any speech or scene; it is a good idea to vary these approaches when working on any part of the plays.

Classroom organization

All these techniques can be used in the classroom, by students sitting at desks or at groups of desks. This is not ideal, but at least all are participating and experiencing the text. The focus here would be on reading and listening.

A space allowing students to sit in a circle encourages more collaborative participation: it focuses attention on the text and on each student in turn, and emphasizes the importance of each individual's contribution.

A space allowing physical movement offers the greatest possibilities. Physicalizing techniques can be used here, marrying physical movement with one or more reading techniques.

Physical work

The following suggestions for physical ways of working on the plays are not all explicitly included in the activities in the book. They are offered here, in outline, for the teacher who may wish to go beyond static reading of the texts, but who does not want students to 'act it out' yet. In all of them, it is assumed that the teacher will be working with a whole class, or large group. The use of the reading techniques described above is implied in these physical activities.

By involving physical movement, these techniques:

- make clear that this is the language of theatre, to be spoken out loud
- release the potential energy of the words, and allow students to experience the power of the language.

Moving to the words

■ Students walk, or run, round the room, reading the chosen piece of text aloud all together. They change direction at every punctuation point, or every sentence, or every end of line. Choose a speed and type of movement to help students experience the energy and rhythms of the verse.

■ The teacher, facing the students standing in their own space in the room, reads the lines aloud, divided into 'sense units'; students repeat the words, and 'show' their meaning at the same time. For example, as they repeat the words, 'Gallop apace, you fiery-footed steeds, towards Phoebus' lodging', for the first time, students might be expected to gallop, to indicate 'fiery steeds' in their movement, and to be puzzled by 'Phoebus' lodging'. Briefly explain 'Phoebus' lodging' and ask them to try again.

Assignments which ask students to visualize and illustrate images and meaning can be started off with this method.

■ Set up physical impediments to the readers. The idea is not to create chaos, but to 'challenge' readers into vocalizing the emotion and energy in the words. In several of these methods, students can be given a line to learn before the activity takes place, so they are not hampered by books as they move about. Some methods are:

a crowd in round one person reading the chosen speech, echoing key words pre-selected by the teacher

b make pairs pull against each other as they read a speech between them

c make one reader of the selected speech do some physical task, for example stacking books, moving from one chair to another on punctuation points

d allocate lines to groups at each end of the room; in order of the lines, students run across the room shouting out their words

e one person reads; one or more students try to stop him or her crossing the room.

More active reading

■ Use the chosen reading approach round the circle; each speaker turns to face the next to say their words.

- Use the chosen reading approach round the circle: each reader walks to the middle of the circle to say their words, if possible with an appropriate gesture to show their meaning.

- As one group of students reads the lines, other students are asked to echo and repeat key words and ideas.

- Vary the pace of any physical activity.

- Vary the volume in reading activities – ask students to use their voice control to whisper, shout, and make appropriate vocal sound effects.

- Work on the words in the verse whose meaning is entirely dependent on context, for example 'here', 'you', 'me', 'that', 'he', 'her', 'she'. These are known as *deictic* words.

Two people reading Paris's and Juliet's interchange –

Paris: Do not deny to *him* that *you* love *me*.
Juliet: *I* will confess to *you* that *I* love *him*.

– highlight these deictic words by pointing to themselves on 'I' and 'me', the other person on 'you', and at Friar Laurence (or an agreed spot in the room) on 'him'. Focusing like this on these words makes their meaning absolutely clear in the specific context. For more complex speeches or interchanges, involving reference to more than one other person, the room can be prepared by pinning up round the walls the names of these characters. As students read, they point to the relevant name, or themselves, on each deictic word. 'Here', 'there', 'up', 'down' and so on can also be treated in this way.

This treatment of deictic words will work whichever reading method has been chosen.

Further active approaches

Additional techniques can be used to increase students' knowledge and understanding of the text.

Acting/presentation

Some activities ask students to act out a scene or part of a scene. This is very useful for students with the confidence to do it, but for others a joint presentation can be preferable.

By using a combination of different reading and physical techniques, students can prepare presentations which involve everyone, without inhibiting those who dislike being 'on show' on their own. One example: in each group some students can be responsible for reading one part between them, while other students work out mimes to accompany the spoken words.

Mime

Mime is useful for students who have yet to gain the confidence to read aloud. It can be developed into 'dumbshow', a mimed presentation of the main action of a scene, or to show the actions of characters as described by others: for example, when Puck describes the flight of the Athenian workmen after Bottom appears with the ass's head; when Benvolio describes two of the street fights; when Casca describes Caesar being offered the crown.

Hotseating, interviewing, interrogating

In each of these activities, a student takes on the role of a character in the play and is questioned about that character's actions, motivation, and thoughts.

In **hotseating**, the whole class or group questions the character. This allows all students to become involved, although they may not all wish to participate.

In **interviewing**, a group or pair, with a specific purpose in mind (producing a newspaper report, television interview, radio interview, other write-up) interviews one person (or each other) in role as a character. Here, each person has a clearly defined part to play.

In **interrogation**, which can be done in groups or pairs, a student in role is put under duress, as in a real interrogation, about their part in the play. Good candidates for this treatment are Brutus, Cassius, and the Tribunes in *Julius Caesar*, Friar Laurence in *Romeo and Juliet*, Puck and Oberon in *A Midsummer Night's Dream*.

Inquest, court hearing

These are more formal frameworks for use when questioning characters, and are described fully where they occur in the activities on the play itself (pages 17–70).

Improvisation

Some assignments ask students to improvise

- the moments before a scene starts
- a similar situation to the one shown in a scene
- action described by a character but not seen on stage.

This can be linked to:

Freeze frames

(This is also know as tableaux, still photographs, or still images.)
In this method, students produce a static representation
designed to reveal the deeper meanings and significance of

- a moment in a scene
- the relationship between a group of characters
- what a character imagines
- images in the text.

Where it is used to represent a moment from a scene, students
can be asked to explain the thoughts and feelings of their
character, and the motivation behind their frozen stance at that
very moment.

Other activities

In addition to active reading techniques and physical activities,
the assignments included in this book offer a wide range of other
tasks intended to encourage and maintain the students'
engagement with the text.

These task are all described where they occur in the activities on
the play (pages 17–70), and include:

Written assignments

Students are invited to produce a wide range of written
responses to the texts. These are well-established in current
classroom practice (many of them can be found listed at the end
of the original Cox Report) and include letters, diaries, point-of-
view writing, accounts of events, students' own playscripts,
letters to and from an agony aunt, newspaper headlines, front
page reports and articles, stream-of-consciousness writing,
dossiers on characters, and obituaries.

Activities based on the play as theatre

Students are asked in some assignments to think about a part of the text as a piece to be staged, reminding them that the texts are above all plays for the theatre.

Students are invited to:

- design the stage set and costumes for a particular scene
- produce sound effects and tape them
- take the director's role, and make decisions about cutting, moving, or changing scenes or parts of scenes
- annotate a script with stage directions for the actors.

Text-based activities

These encourage students to look very closely at the text to:

- select single quotations which sum up whole speeches
- search through an act or the whole play for key images
- present a 'bare bones' or five-minute version of the play by stripping it down to essentials, still using the language of the play.

Showing and sharing

Finally, when students have completed an assignment, they are sometimes invited to share their work with other groups or with the whole class. When the work is active, requiring space and time, thought needs to be given to setting up the classroom for this, and to building in time for reflection, response, and reaction.

Ways in

Characters: names and households

To help you become familiar with the names and relationships of the characters in Romeo and Juliet, play this version of a game called 'Jack to Jill'.

First make labels for these characters, as shown:

Prince Escalus	Mercutio (Prince)	Paris (Prince)
Montague	Lady Montague	Romeo Montague
Benvolio (Montague)	Abram (Montague)	Balthasar(Montague)

Capulet   Lady Capulet   Juliet Capulet
Cousin Capulet   Tybalt (Capulet)   Nurse (Capulet)
Peter (Capulet)   Sampson (Capulet)   Gregory (Capulet)
Friar Laurence   Friar John   Apothecary

(The list shows you who belongs in which household, and who is related to whom.)

If you have more than twenty-one people in the class, add in three Musician labels, and if you have more than twenty-four people, repeat some of the other names.

Each of you has one label, and you all stand in a large circle. To start the game, Prince Escalus crosses the circle to Capulet, saying 'Prince Escalus to Capulet'. Capulet then immediately crosses the circle to someone else, Paris perhaps, saying 'Capulet to Paris'. Paris in turn crosses to someone else, and so on. Always say your own name, and the name of the person you are crossing to. You can make this even more fun by playing it at top speed.

When everyone has had a turn, add in this activity. In turn round the circle, walk to the middle of the circle, say 'I am — and I belong to the — household', and then return to your place. Some characters won't belong to a household, so they must say so.

Then do this further activity: go round the circle in turn, say your name and household, and add in whether you think you are an important character in the play or not. When you move on to the next piece of character work, you will see if you were right.

Character profiles

In the Overview section, on pages 71–75, you will find descriptions of thirteen characters from the play. Follow the suggestions for working on these character descriptions. This will give you a good idea about the characters before you start your work on the play properly.

Themes: opposites

This activity will help you think about some of the main themes in the play. Work in groups of about four, each person in your group taking it in turns to be the modeller. The modeller shapes the rest of the group into a big sculpture to show his or her interpretation of one of the pairs of opposites listed below. When you are the clay or modelling medium, try to be very relaxed and bendy!

power/ authority	powerlessness/obedience
love	hate
violence	peace/friendship
joy/happiness	sorrow/grief

Show one or two of your sculptures to the class, making sure that all four pairs are shown at least once in the class. Discuss with your teacher which sculptures you thought were most effective, and why.

You will now be able to understand more quickly the way opposites run through the play.

Class discussion

Organize a class discussion about the following situation.

Two families have a violent quarrel, which is not settled. It becomes a feud, which goes on for years, with people being killed and injured every time it flares up.

Is this an acceptable way of settling differences?

What part should the law, or the ruler, play in settling the feud?

What should happen to people who kill others during the feud?

You could divide the class into smaller groups or pairs to discuss these questions separately, and then report back your ideas to a whole class discussion. Alternatively, you could discuss the questions in class as a whole group. Get your teacher to help you organize this.

The play

The Prologue briefly outlines the action of the play, in advance. It also highlights three of the main ideas that run through the play: love, violence, and the idea of 'two'.

Love and violence

The prologue makes very clear from the start that the love in the play is a victim of the violence. Make a list of all the words or phrases about love, and another of all the words or phrases about violence. Compare the lengths of your lists.

Two

Two is an important idea in the play because everything springs from the feud between *two* families. The Prologue includes several ways of understanding this word.

Collect all the 'two' words. Decide whether they mean:
- two together, on the same side
- two apart, against each other, one versus one
- two as alternatives, one *or* the other.

 ## Freeze frames

Work in a group to present freeze frames showing the last word in each line: for example, you could show 'mutiny' by showing a group about to overthow a ruler.

Alternatively, draw illustrations for the last word in each line.

Act 1 scene 1

Early on a Sunday morning in mid-July. A street in Verona. The long-standing feud between the Capulets and the Montagues breaks out again, started off by two Capulet servants. Everyone is caught up in this feud. The Prince threatens death to anyone caught fighting in the streets again. Romeo, who has nothing to do with this violence, tells Benvolio about the woman he loves.

Sampson and Gregory   *lines 1–60*

Sampson and Gregory enter in an aggressive mood, and all their words are about violence. Are the serving-men of the Montagues any better?

Read lines 1–60 in fours – three reading the named parts, and one person (Balthasar) joining in with some of Abram's lines. Who would you blame for starting the fight?

Look more closely at these Capulet servants: match their lines with these statements about them:
- they boast about their manhood
- they boast about what they'll do to the men and 'maids' of the Montague household
- they take on the quarrel for their master (the 'ancient grudge' mentioned in the Prologue), and deliberately provoke a fight
- they daren't go beyond the law
- they only get really aggressive when they see Tybalt coming ('one of my master's kinsmen', line 55, is Tybalt).

With your partner, discuss your opinion of these two serving-men. Share with the class:
- your opinion of Sampson and Gregory
- the best three or four words you can think of to describe them
- your suggestions about modern equivalents of Sampson and Gregory.

Other characters get involved   *lines 61–112*

Benvolio, as his name suggests ('well-wishing'), is peaceful and tries to stop the fight. But Sampson and Gregory know their man: when Tybalt arrives on the scene he challenges Benvolio, instead of stopping the brawl.

With your partner, look at Benvolio's lines from line 61 to line 112, and decide if his name suits him.

Look at Tybalt's words in lines 67–68, and decide what you think of his reasons for fighting. Have you any sympathy with them?

The Prince and law and order   *lines 79–101*

Prince Escalus, as the ruler of Verona, is now faced with the results of this feud which he has not stopped. Later in the play he says he 'winked at their discords'.

Work in groups of four or five. Use the Prince's speech, lines 79–101, as the basis for a newspaper feature called 'Riot and Disorder in Verona'. Include the following items:

- an interview with the Prince: make him account for his action (and inaction!), and face up to the disobedience of his subjects
- an eyewitness account of the brawl
- a report on the Montagues and Capulets, their long-standing feud, and recommendations for what the Prince should do about it
- comments from local citizens.

Before you start, decide what kind of newspaper you are producing, and what kind of readers will be reading it.

 ## Montague and Lady Montague   *lines 114–153*

Lady Montague asks Benvolio about Romeo. Romeo's parents are very concerned about him but they know that he won't talk to them. They never speak to their son in the play.

Work with a partner. Make a note of the words spoken by Montague which indicate that he is very disturbed by Romeo's behaviour.

Improvise a discussion between Romeo's parents about their son's behaviour, and their worries about him.

Turn your improvisation into a short playscript, in modern English. Lines 116–151 contain the vital information!

Romeo in love   *lines 154–236*

In the rest of this scene, lines 154–236, Romeo talks about his misery. Love brings suffering, not happiness, to Romeo.

Write Romeo's letter to an agony aunt, and her reply to him. Use all the information Romeo gives about himself and the woman he loves (called Rosaline) in your letters. Show how miserable and powerless Romeo feels. Can the agony aunt offer him any hope?

Act 1 scene 2

Sunday afternoon, Verona.
Paris comes to the Capulet house to ask to marry Juliet. Capulet is in no hurry to see her married, and tells him to wait for two years. He invites Paris to an 'old accustomed feast', so that Paris can see Juliet for the first time. Benvolio sees the feast as an opportunity of getting Romeo to forget Rosaline, and encourages him to go.

Juliet's father, Capulet   *lines 7–19*

Work with a partner. Read lines 7–19 between you. Discuss and then note down:

- what information Capulet gives about Juliet and about himself
- what kind of father you think he is at this point.

Benvolio   *lines 82–99*

Why does Benvolio suggest they go to the feast? What do you
think of his suggestion? He doesn't seem to see any harm in
going to a *Capulet* feast, in spite of what Tybalt said to him that
morning. Is he being careless? Asking for trouble? Fed up with
Romeo? Note down your answers to these questions.

Act 1 scene 3

Sunday, late afternoon. Capulet's house in Verona.
Juliet appears for the first time, with her mother and her nurse.
Her mother talks to her about marriage to Paris, and her nurse
shows great enthusiasm for the idea, although Juliet herself has
never yet thought about marriage.

The Nurse and Juliet   *lines 17–57*

The Nurse has so much to say and so many memories! She talks
about Juliet in a way that her mother never does; after all, she
has cared for her since she was born.

Work with a partner. Read lines 17–48 and 50–57 between you
as fast as you can, changing over at punctuation marks, trying to
express the Nurse's enjoyment in
your tone of voice.

Suggest why she finds her memory
of Juliet and her husband so
funny, and make a note of all the
information she gives about Juliet.

Storyboard or write the story of
that day, eleven years ago, when
Juliet fell over, bringing out the
Nurse's enjoyment and her
relationship with her husband.

Which moment from Act 1 scene 2
do you think this is showing?

Lady Capulet and Juliet *lines 81–92*

Lady Capulet speaks to her daughter in a very formal way, as she describes Paris within the conventional form of a sonnet, comparing him to a book.

Imagine you are Juliet listening to this description. What picture of Paris does it give you? Do you feel attracted to him? What do you think your mother is trying to do? Talk through your answers to these questions with your partner.

Keep the sonnet or not? *lines 74–99*

Work with a partner. In the first version of *Romeo and Juliet*, printed in 1599 in an edition called the 'First Quarto', Lady Capulet's sonnet about Paris does not appear at all. Instead of your lines 74–99 there are these:

Lady Capulet:	Well girl, the noble County Paris seeks thee for his wife.
Nurse:	A man young lady, lady such a man as all the world, why he is a man of wax.
Lady Capulet:	Verona's summer hath not such a flower.
Nurse:	Nay he is a flower, in faith a very flower.
Lady Capulet:	Well Juliet, how like you of Paris' love?
Juliet:	I'll look to like, if looking liking move, But no more deep will I engage mine eye Than your consent gives strength to make it fly. *(Exeunt)*

Three volunteers act out both versions of this part of the scene to the whole class. Your teacher will need to help with this! Then in pairs, discuss the different effects of the two versions and report back your opinions.

Then half the class, in pairs, prepare an argument in favour of keeping the sonnet in a performance of the play, while the other half of the class, in pairs, prepare an argument against keeping the sonnet in. Then, as a whole class, listen to the arguments for and against, and decide which you support.

Thee/thou/you – your ideas

Work with a partner. What did you notice about what Lady Capulet, the Nurse, and Juliet call each other in this scene?

Copy out this table and complete it either with 'you' or with 'thee/thou':

Lady Capulet calls Juliet .... and the Nurse ....

The Nurse calls Lady Capulet .... and Juliet ....

Juliet calls Lady Capulet .... and the Nurse ....

Discuss your explanation for the use of these different words. What do they indicate about relationships between the three characters? Do your own research into this, and see if you can relate this to what you know of French or German.

Juliet going to the feast   *lines 97–105*

Work on your own. Read the last lines which Juliet (lines 97–99), Lady Capulet (line 104), and the Nurse (line 105) say in the scene: what expectations for Juliet do they each have about the feast? List your findings.

Act 1 scene 4

Sunday evening, a street in Verona.
Romeo, Benvolio, and Mercutio are on their way to the Capulet feast. This is Mercutio's first appearance, and his light-heartedness contrasts with Romeo's misery and deep misgivings. Mercutio makes fun of his fears and talks about Queen Mab, the fairies' midwife, instead.

Romeo's misery and foreboding   *lines 1–53*

With a partner, look at lines 1–53 and find the words which show that
- Romeo is still very depressed, and seems convinced that his death will result from going to the feast

■   Mercutio (a kinsman of the Prince) is trying to joke Romeo out of his misery.

 ### Mercutio and Queen Mab   *lines 53–94*

Romeo has had a dream, but Mercutio doesn't ask to hear it. He goes off into a long fantasy about Queen Mab, the fairies' midwife who brings dreams to birth.

Work on his Queen Mab speech in two sections: first, in groups of six, read lines 53–69 by punctuation marks in 'tiny' voices to convey the minute scale of Queen Mab.

Then, for lines 70–88, have three readers and three mime partners: each reader has a mime partner. As each person reads all the lines about one of the people Mercutio describes, the mime partner mimes the actions described by Mercutio.

For lines 88–94, where Mercutio describes other actions of Queen Mab, experiment with different ways of saying the words: loudly, softly, threateningly, laughingly. Divide up the words and lines between you to make the greatest impact. What idea of Queen Mab do these words give you? Make your reading of them fit your ideas.

 ### *Put the speech together*

Your teacher will need to help here, because this works best if you have photocopied sheets of the speech which you can mark with pen or pencil. Building on what you have already done, put together a whole class performance of this speech. Use mime, voice pitch and expression, echoing and repetition of lines and words, sound effects, sharing out the reading between you. Be ambitious! Learn your words, and try a whole class performance without the script.

This is she –   *line 94*

Discuss with a partner what kind of thing Mercutio was going to say when Romeo stopped him. Why did Romeo stop him?

Mercutio

When you have done these assignments, discuss with your class what conclusions you can draw about Mercutio from his words.

The masquers

The host of a feast in the sixteenth century was flattered if masquers arrived uninvited. As Benvolio suggests, they would dance, pay compliments to the host and then depart, with no harm done. Benvolio says, 'We'll measure them a measure, and be gone' – he does not expect to be there long.

Design (and make if you can!) animal or bird masks for Romeo, Benvolio, and Mercutio, choosing one that fits your idea of their character.

Act 1 scene 5

Sunday night. The Capulet feast, Verona.
This is the scene in which Romeo and Juliet meet for the first time. The whole situation is likely to bring disaster in the future, but they know nothing of that now. Tybalt's anger at Romeo's presence is only kept in control for the time being.

Staging the feast scene   *lines 1–143*

Work as a whole class divided into suitable groups. This scene is full of activity, and the meeting of Romeo and Juliet is only a small part of it. These divisions will help you:

lines 1–15:	the servants are busy.
lines 16–29:	the guests arrive and are welcomed by Capulet.
lines 30–40:	Capulet talks to his old cousin about the past.
lines 41–52:	Romeo sees Juliet and speaks about her beauty.
lines 53–91:	Tybalt overhears Romeo, and sends for his rapier to kill him, but Capulet stops him. He departs, swearing revenge.

lines 92–110:   Romeo takes Juliet's hand, speaks to her and kisses her.

lines 111–119:   Romeo asks the Nurse who Juliet is, and is shocked to discover she's a Capulet.

lines 120–126:   Capulet says farewell to his guests.

lines 127–143:   Juliet is shocked to discover that Romeo is a Montague.

 Try presenting the scene in one of the following ways, with everyone in the class involved.

Acting

Present the scene in sections, with separate groups taking charge of each section. Your groups may need to be flexible to cope with the whole scene.

Freeze frames

Each group works out one freeze frame showing a key moment in their section.

Improvisation

From the outline given above, each group improvises one section.

Put the whole scene together, for a grand presentation. With your teacher discuss some of the problems you found as you worked on this.

 ### Capulet and Tybalt   *lines 53–91*

In lines 53–91, Tybalt and Capulet get very angry with each other, Tybalt because Romeo is at the Capulet feast, and Capulet because Tybalt is defying him.

Work in pairs, reading the lines in parts, using your voices and physical movements to show clearly what your feelings are. Now tell each other what you are angry about.

Romeo and Juliet   *lines 41–52*

Romeo first sees Juliet at line 41. He doesn't know she is a Capulet. He compares her to bright torches, a rich jewel, a white dove amongst black crows, and says, 'I ne'er saw true beauty till this night'.

Do you remember how much Romeo loved Rosaline (in Act 1 scenes 1 and 2)? How do you react to his sudden change of love? Can you explain it? How seriously do you take it?

 ## A sonnet   *lines 92–109*

Romeo and Juliet speak the words of a sonnet as they meet. Romeo talks to Juliet as though she were holy, a divine being. She replies using the same kinds of words. Their words are about religious people: their meaning is love.

Work out from their words what movements their hands and lips are making; you can either work with another pair, having two people miming while two others read, or work with your own partner, making your own movements.

Diaries

In this scene, many things happen which could lead to important future events. Write diary entries for Capulet, Tybalt, Romeo, or Juliet, as they reflect on what happened to them at the feast, and what may happen next.

Juliet   *lines 137–142*

Work with a partner. At the end of the scene Juliet discovers who Romeo is. It is already too late – she cannot stop loving him.

When the Nurse overhears her words in lines 137–140 and asks 'What's this, what's this?', Juliet's reply is 'A rhyme I learn'd even now of one I danc'd withal'. Is this a lie? Would Juliet feel the need to lie about Romeo to the Nurse?

Act 2 scene 1

Sunday night, after the feast, in the street outside Capulet's orchard, Verona.

Romeo cannot bear to leave Juliet's house. When Mercutio and Benvolio call him he doesn't answer. Mercutio conjures him to appear, as a magician would, and uses the name and body of Rosaline to conjure by. He doesn't know that her name has no effect on Romeo any longer – Romeo is in love with Juliet. Mercutio and Benvolio give up and go home to bed.

Act 2 scene 2

Sunday night through to dawn on Monday. Capulet's orchard and house, Verona.
In this long scene, one of the most famous in all Shakespeare's plays, Romeo and Juliet meet again. Juliet proposes marriage to Romeo, who agrees to tell her messenger the next morning what arrangements he has made. The scene shows how different they are, in thought, language, and experience.

All the assignments here will help you understand the language of the scene. Before you do them, read the whole scene aloud round the class, then split into smaller groups or pairs for this work. Afterwards you can try a performance of the scene using everything you have learned.

It is the East and Juliet is the sun   *lines 1–32*

Romeo has only seen Juliet at night. When he sees her at her window, she appears to him to be a source of light herself: for him she is so beautiful that the only worthy things to compare her with are the sun, moon and stars. He is looking up, not just at her but at the sky – so the heavenly bodies are natural points of comparison.

With a partner, write down everything Romeo says about Juliet's 'lightness'. (Look back at what he said when he first saw her at the feast, Act 1 scene 5 lines 43–52).

One way of making Romeo's images 'visible' is to try to draw them. Try your hand at illustrations for lines 3, 15–18, 20–22.

She speaks – her words   *lines 33–49*

Juliet's words follow a logical argument. She attempts to find a way out of the impossible situation she realizes she is in. She sees the problem as one of names. Her line of reasoning goes like this:

Why are you Romeo? (because that makes you my enemy).
Refuse to be a Montague (because then you won't be my enemy).
If you won't do that, I'll stop being a Capulet (then I won't be your enemy).
It's only your name that is my enemy (not you yourself).
You would still be you, even if your name wasn't Montague.
What is that name Montague?
It isn't any physical part of a man.
Be another name. (Call yourself by another name.)
What is in a name?
Romeo would still be perfect, even if he were not called Romeo.
Take off your name.
Take all of me in exchange.

Work with a partner to:
■   match up these statements with the words she actually says
■   discuss Juliet's reasoning: does it make sense to you?

Juliet is trying to separate the name from the person. But look back at what has been said so far in the play about the names Montague and Capulet. It has been made very clear that there is no escaping your name and what it stands for.

Can you shed your name, and become someone else? Will Juliet's idea work? Talk about this with your partner.

Art thou not Romeo, and a Montague?   *lines 60–84*

Work with a partner. Look at what is going on between Romeo and Juliet in these lines. Juliet asks Romeo serious questions which show her fear for his safety. Read the lines between you to see what Romeo replies to these lines of Juliet's:

> How cam'st thou hither, tell me, and wherefore? *plus the next 3 lines* (lines 62–65)

If they do see thee they will murder thee (line 70)
I would not for the world they saw thee here (line 74)
By whose direction found'st thou out this place? (line 79)

Decide between you what you think of Romeo's replies. Is he taking Juliet seriously? Read the lines again, trying to use your voices to show their attitudes.

Dost thou love me?   *lines 95–105*

Juliet already knows that her love for Romeo is deep and dependable. Find and write down the five statements she makes in lines 95–105 which show how strong her love is.

These photographs show two different moments in the balcony scene, from two different productions. Can you identify the moments? Do you prefer the more traditional or the modern staging?

Juliet

lines 85-106

What conclusions about Juliet could you draw from her words in lines 85–106? Discuss your ideas with your partner.

Romeo's reply

lines 107–115

When Juliet asks Romeo 'Dost thou love me?' he has to wait before he can answer. Look at his words at lines 107–108, 112, 115. Does he ever answer her question? What does he do instead?

Thy purpose marriage

lines 85–150

Juliet takes control of the dialogue from line 85. Up to her first exit, after line 138, she is talking of her great love for Romeo, and the exchange of love vows. When she reappears, at line 141, she talks of marriage.

With a partner, work out three or four reasons to account for Juliet's proposing marriage to Romeo so soon after meeting him.

All this is but a dream

lines 139–141

Do you remember the dream Romeo had before the feast, which worried him? This *real* experience with Juliet seems to him like

another dream. Why? With your partner, list everything which makes him doubt the reality of what is happening to him.

This is supposed to be the balcony in Verona where the 'balcony scene' really took place. Does it fit with your idea of the setting?

Love

Look back through the scene and collect all the lines which express Romeo's and Juliet's love for each other. List them separately. Compare your lists with your partner's.

Act 2 scene 3

Early Monday morning. Friar Lawrence's cell, Verona. Friar Laurence, Romeo's confessor, agrees to marry Romeo and Juliet in order to bring about a reconciliation between the two households. His relationship with Romeo mirrors that of the Nurse with Juliet. Friar Laurence's skill with herbs and plants, as well as his Christianity, gives him an insight into the good and bad in human beings as well as in nature.

Baleful weeds and precious-juiced flowers   *lines 1–26*

Friar Laurence is an expert on the poisons and medicines which can be made from plants and herbs. His words in lines 1–26 express the idea of good and bad existing side by side in nature.

Make a simple table of two columns, 'good' and 'bad', to help you sort out what he is saying. Enter the appropriate words and phrases from his lines in each column.

Friar Laurence believes that the 'two opposed kings' who 'encamp them' in man are 'grace' (capacity to receive divine grace, blessedness) and 'rude will' (the impulse to give way to the desires of the flesh): he compares these 'opposed kings' to the two 'encamped' in 'this weak flower': 'poison' and 'medicine'. ('Grace' and 'rude will' are a more complicated way of thinking of 'good' and 'bad'.)

'My ghostly father'   *lines 61–84*

The form of address between Friar Laurence and Romeo is 'thou/thee', like that between Juliet and the Nurse, which shows a friendly, informal relationship. In lines 61–84, Friar Laurence talks about recent conversations between himself and Romeo, about Romeo's love for Rosaline. He doesn't sound very sympathetic.

Work with a partner. Using the information in lines 61–84, and trying to use 'thee/thou' as you talk to each other, improvise a short scene between you in which Romeo tells Friar Laurence how much he loves Rosaline, and Friar Laurence gives him the best advice he can. (Look back to Act 1 scene 1 lines 200–235 to remind yourself why Rosaline will not give in to Romeo.)

For doting, not for loving   *line 78*

Work with a partner. What do you think Friar Laurence means by these words? Would he say that Romeo is still doting? What would he call Juliet's feelings for Romeo? What words would you use to talk about 'doting' nowadays? Discuss your ideas about 'doting' and 'loving', and note them down.

'Her I love now'

Are you surprised at Romeo's words at line 82? Is the only reason he loves Juliet because she loves him? What do you think? Put one of the class in the hot seat, as Romeo, and question him closely about his love for Juliet, using what he has said up to this point to help you with your questions. To get you started, you could consider whether

- he loves her because she is beautiful
- he loves her because she loves him
- he loves her because he would love anybody who responded to him.

Act 2 scene 4

Monday morning, before midday. A street in Verona.
Romeo jokes with his friends, meets the Nurse, and tells her the arrangements for the marriage. As a forewarning of what might happen, Tybalt has sent a challenge to Romeo. This is the only scene in which Romeo talks cheerfully with his friends.

Rosaline torments him so   *lines 4–92*

Mercutio and Benvolio don't know about Romeo's love for
Juliet, and neither of them ever finds out. Mercutio thinks it's
still Rosaline he loves, and that he's been driven mad by her.

Work with a partner. Read lines 4–5, 13–17, and 87–92, and
discuss and note down what you think Mercutio's views of love
are. Include in your notes particular words or phrases used by
Mercutio which sum up his attitude.

 Improvise a short scene with your partner in which Romeo first
told Mercutio he was in love with Rosaline. Use what Romeo
says in Act 1 scene 1, and what Mercutio says in this scene to
help you.

You will see that Romeo does not tell Mercutio anything about
Juliet (lines 50–52). Can you suggest why not?

Mercutio and Tybalt   *lines 28–36*

Mercutio reacts to the news that Tybalt has sent a challenge to
Romeo at his father's house by wondering whether Romeo is a
'man to encounter Tybalt'. He is joking about it, but it's worth
remembering this casual remark later in the play when Romeo
and Tybalt meet. Look back to Act 1 scene 5 to see why Tybalt
has sent a challenge to Romeo.

Why does Mercutio think Romeo is already as good as dead (line
13)?

Romeo and Mercutio   *lines 47–97*

Mercutio and Romeo go in for some friendly fencing with words
in these lines, and quite a lot of what they say is sexually
suggestive. Mercutio wants to know where Romeo has been, and
Romeo cleverly avoids answering him.

Work in groups of seven or eight. Three of you read Mercutio's,
Romeo's, and Benvolio's lines while the rest of the group make
noises of encouragement, booing and so on, to indicate which
one of them is winning the 'fight', and to indicate which of their

words you find funny, clever, and suggestive. Read the lines fairly quickly, keeping a good speed up. You might need to do this more than once to get an enjoyable performance going.

Look out for the following words (the double meaning in many of them is not hard to guess!) and make your noisy reactions when you hear them:

> slip, counterfeit, conceive, case, strain, curtsy, kindly, exposition, pink, courtesy, flower, pump, single, singular, match, goose, bite thy ear, bite, bitter, sweeting, sharp sauce, sweet goose, broad, natural, bauble, hole, hair, tale, large, argument.

Mercutio

Mercutio says, 'Why, is this not better now than groaning for love? . . . Now art thou Romeo; now art thou what thou art, by art as well as by nature.' Mercutio, as his name suggests (mercury: quicksilver) is quick-witted, emotional, capable of violence, and likely to explode with anger. He likes Romeo to be 'one of the lads', not miserable because he's in love. He talks about sex rather than love, and often his words are not just suggestive, but crude and obvious.

Irony

This term is a useful shorthand way of describing a situation where the audience, and/or other characters on stage, know something which changes the significance of what the original speaker is saying. The irony in what Mercutio says – 'Is this not better now than groaning for love?' – is that it is love, responded to and returned, which has made Romeo as cheerful as he is. Romeo, of course, says nothing in reply to Mercutio.

 ## A shirt and a smock　　　　　　　　　*lines 99–140*

Mercutio teases the Nurse when she appears, but does Romeo join in?

Work in groups of five or more. Act out this section of the scene (lines 99–140). Each person in the group take one of the parts:

the Nurse, Peter, Mercutio, Romeo, and Benvolio. If you have a bigger group, you can have other people watching the teasing.

Before you start acting, read the lines through to get a feel of the scene.

Decide:

- what Peter and Benvolio should be doing, as they have no lines to speak
- what Mercutio has found, or seen, when he cries out 'So ho!' (line 126). All his words to and about the Nurse indicate that he thinks she is a loose woman, a bawd or prostitute
- how Romeo reacts to Mercutio's teasing of the Nurse.

When you have put together your mini-performance, show it to the class and compare the solutions each group came to about Peter, Benvolio, and Romeo.

In your group come up with an answer to these questions:
- Why didn't Romeo stop Mercutio?
- What opinion do you have of Romeo in this scene?

In one way Mercutio's behaviour and the Nurse's reaction are funny. In your group discuss whether you think there is another side to it, and note down your ideas.

 ### 'My mistress is the sweetest lady'   *lines 106–206*

Work in groups of three or four. Using lines 106–158, 161–170, and 194–207, set up an interview with the Nurse, one of you in role as the Nurse, the rest of the group as interviewers. Ask her about her feelings for Juliet, about why and how she's helping Juliet to marry Romeo, and about Mercutio's treatment of her. Note down her answers.

Act 2 scene 5

Monday, midday. Capulet's house.
The Nurse tells Juliet the arrangements for the marriage. By holding back the news she makes Juliet very impatient. This scene echoes the scene between Romeo and Friar Laurence.

'Love's heralds should be thoughts' *lines 1–15*

Work as a whole class, or as two big groups. To experience something of Juliet's impatience, do the following exercise.

Read lines 1–15 standing in a circle, changing readers at each punctuation point. For the second reading, turn to face the next person as you say your words; turn the other way to 'receive' the words spoken to you. The third time (you will be becoming more familiar with the words and rhythm by now) pass a soft ball on from reader to reader round the circle. The fourth time, spread the circle wider, and throw the ball from reader to reader. As you gain confidence you can think of your own variations; it is possible, with practice, to do this in pairs!

'I am aweary' *lines 18–64*

Work in groups of three or four. Is the Nurse really weary or is she teasing Juliet? Try two ways of looking at this part of the scene, first reading lines 18–64 round your group as though the Nurse is really teasing, then reading the lines seriously. Listen carefully to the two different interpretations, and decide which one is most convincing.

Form of address

The Nurse addresses Juliet here as 'you': can you suggest why she has changed from Act 1 scene 3, where she called her 'thee/thou'? Juliet still calls her 'thee/thou': can you think of any reason? Refer back to page 23.

 ### Freeze frames *lines 18–65*

Work with a partner. Devise a freeze frame to capture the actions and expressions of the Nurse and Juliet at one moment during this part of the scene. Show your freeze frame to the class, who have to work out which line it shows.

Add one more element to this activity: when you have guessed the correct line for each freeze frame, ask the Nurse and Juliet what thoughts are going through their minds at that precise moment.

Act 2 scene 6

Monday afternoon. Friar Lawrence's cell, Verona.
Romeo and Juliet meet at Friar Laurence's cell. Friar Laurence,
marrying them secretly but with the best of intentions, will not
leave them alone together until they have been properly married
in the sight of God.

The language of love   *lines 24–34*

Work with a partner. How do Romeo and Juliet express their
love? Read lines 24–34 between you. Pick out the key words they
each use about their love.

Make a poster for display to represent the love of Romeo and
Juliet, using your key words, with illustrations (drawn by you or
taken from magazines).

Discuss your reaction to these words. Do they surprise you or do
you find nothing unusual about them?

Foreboding   *lines 1–15*

Work with a partner. Both Romeo and Friar Laurence express
fears about the future in lines 1–15. Collect their words or
phrases. Make a poster using your words and illustrations to
show these fears. Display it alongside your 'Language of love'
poster.

Another version   *lines 16–37*

Shakespeare probably rewrote some parts of *Romeo and Juliet*.
This is an earlier version of the last part of this scene, when Juliet
arrives (lines 16–37):

> *(Juliet enters somewhat fast, and embraceth Romeo)*
> Friar: See where she comes.
>   So light of foot ne'er hurts the trodden flower:
>   Of love and joy, see, see the sovereign power.
> Juliet: Romeo.
> Romeo: Juliet, welcome. As do waking eyes,
>   Closed in night's mists, attend the frolic day,

	So Romeo hath expected Juliet,
	And thou art come.
Juliet:	I am, if I be day,
	Come to my sun: shine forth and make me fair.
Romeo:	All beauteous fairness dwelleth in thine eyes.
Juliet:	Romeo from thine all brightness doth arise.
Friar:	Come wantons, come, the stealing hours do pass.
	Defer embracements till some fitter time,
	Part for a while, you shall not be alone,
	Till holy church have joined you both in one.
Romeo:	Lead, holy Father, all delay seems long.
Juliet:	Make haste, make haste, this lingering doth us
	wrong.
Friar:	O, soft and fair makes sweetest work they say.
	Haste is a common hinderer in cross way.

The extracts are about the same length, 19 lines in the earlier
and 22 in the later. They seem quite different in many ways.

Divide the class in two: each half prepares a reading of one
version. Practise until you feel confident, sharing out the reading
round the group. Listen to each reading. You may need to do
this more than once.

Discuss as a class what differences you noticed and which
version you prefer.

Work with a partner to produce a short set of recommendations
for the older version to be used in a production instead of the
usual one. The notes below might help you, as you weigh up the
effectiveness of one set of images against the other.

In the earlier version, many of the words are about light (and its
opposite, dark), sight and eyes, and time

sight/eyes/light/dark	see, see
time	expected
see	waking eyes
attend	stealing hours

In the later version, the words are more to do with
worth/wealth/amount, as well as with love.

worth/wealth	joy	heaped
love	measure	love
much	happiness	rich

Act 3 scene 1

Monday afternoon, an hour or so after the marriage. A street in Verona.
This scene is the turning point of the play. Before Romeo arrives, the events which will lead to his banishment have already been sparked off. His friend Mercutio and his 'new' cousin Tybalt are killed, and all the promise of his marriage to Juliet is destroyed.

The assignments that follow deal with each part of the scene separately. When you have finished working on them, you might decide to put all your work together to give a class presentation of the scene.

 ### These hot days   *lines 1–30*

Work with a partner. Mercutio describes the kind of trivial incident that can spark off a fight. He mentions six: in the tavern, the man with the beard, the man cracking nuts, the man coughing in the street, the tailor and his doublet, the tailor and the shoes. Are any of these really worth fighting about?

Either work out an improvisation, or draw a set of storyboards for one of these incidents, and give your verdict on the kind of people who would get involved in such fights.

Do you agree with these statements about Benvolio and Mercutio?

■ Neither Mercutio nor Benvolio have so far appeared to be quarrelsome.
■ Mercutio has been more likely to tease and enjoy word-play.
■ Benvolio has been a peacemaker, and a looker-on.

 ### Apt to quarrel   *lines 35–58*

Work in groups of six. You learned in Act 2 scene 4 (earlier that day) how much Mercutio dislikes Tybalt. Make sure you understand lines 35–58, then have two people for each of the characters in the scene: one to read the lines, the other to 'thought shadow'. To do this, each reader stops when they have read each speech to allow their 'thought shadow' to speak aloud the thoughts that might be going through their minds. For example:

| Benvolio: | By my head, here comes the Capulets. |
| Thought shadow: | The very people I don't want to see, I hope there's no trouble. |

Then act the lines out, without the thought shadows, using what you learned from them to give your performance energy and conviction.

Work out what Tybalt and Mercutio each want out of this encounter, and note down your thoughts.

 ## Here comes my man   *lines 59–74*

Work in groups of four. Why does Tybalt call Romeo 'villain' (line 60)? Is this justified? (Look back at Act 1 scene 5 lines 60–91 for Tybalt's reason.)

Romeo refuses to rise to Tybalt's insult, even though Tybalt twice tries to provoke him.

In your groups of four, read and act out lines 59–74, preparing your work first by:

■ deciding what are the stage directions indicated in the words:

Therefore farewell; I see thou know'st me not (line 64)
Therefore turn and draw (line 67)
. . . be satisfied (line 71)

■ deciding what Romeo and Tybalt are doing while Mercutio speaks at lines 72–74

■ considering what prompts Mercutio to speak: is it simply that Romeo has refused a fight, or for other reasons?

Show your finished performance to the class.

What would'st thou have with me?   *lines 55–82*

In pairs, discuss why Tybalt takes up Mercutio's challenge at line 81. Why doesn't he go after Romeo? How does Mercutio make sure that Tybalt must answer him? Note down your thoughts.

What is Mercutio fighting about? Tybalt's insults to Romeo – 'consort', 'boy', or 'villain'? Or Romeo's 'calm, dishonourable, vile submission'? Improvise with your partner and then write down the thoughts that flash through Mercutio's mind as he watches Tybalt and Romeo exchange words.

In this photograph of Mercutio and Tybalt fighting, can you work out which of the onlookers is Romeo?

I was hurt under your arm   *lines 83–108*

Some modern editions of the play use a stage direction which comes from the first edition of the play (the First Quarto) after line 88: 'Tybalt under Romeo's arm thrusts Mercutio'.

Work in groups of three. Act out lines 83–90, performing the movements in slow motion. Show clearly your interpretation of the wounding of Mercutio: was it deliberate or a mistake? Show clearly the part Romeo plays in it.

Read lines 90–108. Decide at what point Romeo realizes that Mercutio is telling the truth about his wound. Write down the thoughts that flash through Romeo's mind as he listens to Mercutio say,

'Why the devil came you between us?
I was hurt under your arm.'
(lines 101–103)

Your houses!

Mercutio's curse on the two houses, spoken as he is dying, and repeated three times, is certain to be fulfilled.

This day's black fate   *lines 109–136*

Work with a partner. Benvolio tells Romeo that Mercutio is dead. The sight of Tybalt is enough to make Romeo forget his own words, 'the Prince expressly hath forbid this bandying in Verona streets', and to turn on him with 'fire-ey'd fury'. Tybalt is a more practised swordsman than he: fury gives Romeo the upper hand.

Write down all the words from lines 109–126 in which Romeo expresses his anger.

Discuss what Romeo means when he says: 'O, I am Fortune's fool'. How has Fortune made a fool of him? Fortune was a common way of talking about fate, luck, the stars or destiny in Shakespeare's time. In pictures, Fortune was usually shown as a woman with a huge upright wheel on which people were fixed. As Fortune turned her wheel, they moved round it: in life they might be at the height of fortune one minute and at the bottom the next.

Try out different ways of saying this line: angrily? Regretfully? Miserably? Shouting? Whispering?

 ### The Prince

Work in groups of five or more. The Prince has to face several problems:
- he has himself already forbidden any more brawling in the streets, on pain of death
- Lady Capulet is demanding Romeo's life as the price for Tybalt's death
- his kinsman Mercutio has been one of the victims
- and, as he says himself:

> Romeo slew him; he slew Mercutio.
> Who now the price of his dear blood doth owe?

He decides on a compromise: he banishes Romeo.

In your group divide into two pairs: one pair prepare and make a case supporting the Prince's decision, the other pair prepare and make a case for the execution of Romeo. Set up your mini-debate formally, with a chairperson controlling the proceedings and each side listening to what the other has to say before any further discussion is allowed. At the end, try to reach agreement!

Romeo

Work with a partner. Look through the whole scene, and find the lines which match these statements about Romeo, tracing his emotional changes in the scene. When you have found the line, decide on one word that describes his mood at that moment and write it down.

1 He's just married Juliet.

2 He genuinely doesn't know what Tybalt wants with him – he does not know that Tybalt saw him at the Capulet feast and was prevented from attacking him.

3 He gives the best answer he can to the challenge – and it is true.

4 He does not expect Mercutio to step in and fight for him – in fact he has no way of knowing that he has walked into a situation which is already on the boil.

5 He tries to stop the fight – unsuccessfully.

6 He doesn't realize that Mercutio is wounded to death. When he does, he knows what he must do, and has to throw off his gentle behaviour (he talks of Juliet having made him effeminate). He realizes that he will have to fight for two reasons: to redeem his reputation, and to avenge Mercutio's death.

Romeo in control?

Work with a partner. Look back over the play so far, and note down all the events in which Romeo has been involved (the Capulet feast, meeting Juliet, the balcony scene, marriage to Juliet, the street fight with Tybalt). Add your comments about which of these events Romeo has had any control over.

Act 3 scene 2

Monday evening. Capulet's house, Verona.
Romeo and Juliet have been married for about three hours.
Juliet knows nothing of what happened outside in the street, and
is eagerly awaiting the night. The joyful mood at the start of the
scene changes suddenly to misery when the Nurse brings the
news of Tybalt's death. Juliet's love for Romeo is really put to
the test.

Love-performing night　　　　　　*lines 1–31*

Juliet urges night to come so that she can sleep with Romeo on
this night of their wedding. Her words are full of desire which
she expresses through the idea of night.

Work as a class. Read lines 1–31 round the class, by punctuation
marks. One group of six does not read but instead echoes all the
words to do with night as the rest of the group reads. Try
different ways of reading this: whispering, dreamily, urgently,
impatiently. Then make a note of all these words.

He's dead, he's dead, he's dead!　　　*lines 36–70*

The Nurse says straight out what is on her mind, not preparing
Juliet for her news. A feature of her speech is to go off the point
and not to say at once everything she knows. In Act 2 scene 5
she was possibly teasing, here she is grief-stricken.

Work in groups of four. Two of you read the Nurse's lines only
from 36–70. After each set of lines, the other two speak out loud
the ideas her words are bound to put into Juliet's head. How
long does the Nurse keep Juliet guessing?

The whole group now reads all the lines, two of you sharing the
Nurse's lines, two of you sharing Juliet's. How close to Juliet's
actual words were you as you did the previous activity?

Juliet   *lines 73–85*

How can Juliet come to terms with what has happened? Her 'dearest cousin' has been killed by her 'dearer lord': how could Romeo's hand shed Tybalt's blood?

She expresses her conflicting emotions by putting conflicting ideas together. Contradictory ideas put side by side are called 'oxymorons' – from two Greek words, *oxus* (sharp) and *moros* (stupid).

With a partner, read lines 73–85, changing over at each punctuation mark. Practise using a harsh voice for the 'bad' things and a gentle voice for the 'good' things she mentions. Read the lines again, this time one of you reading all the 'bad' words and the other all the 'good' words.

 Also make up freeze frames of two or three of her oxymorons. Show them to other pairs, and see if they can work out which ones you are showing.

Blistered be thy tongue for such a wish! *lines 90–95*

Juliet cannot sort out this terrible problem, but the Nurse's next words, 'Shame come to Romeo!', make her realize immediately where her loyalties now lie.

Work with a partner. Take parts for lines 90–95. Make the Nurse sound angry and Juliet even angrier – have them shouting at each other. Swap parts and do it again. Work out other ways of making these words sound powerful – maybe hissing them? Quiet but intense? Discuss what makes Juliet so angry.

Wherefore weep I then?   *lines 100–126*

Juliet temporarily forgets the key word in what the Nurse said: banishment. Look at what Juliet says when she remembers it: how does she interpret that word?

I'll find Romeo   *lines 127–143*

The Nurse becomes more comforting towards Juliet, and takes a ring for Romeo; she knows he is at Friar Laurence's cell. In pairs, read lines 127–143 between you.

At line 90 the Nurse said, 'Shame come to Romeo'; at line 138 she says, 'I'll find Romeo to comfort you'. What do you think makes her change her attitude?

Act 3 scene 3

Monday evening. Friar Laurence's cell, Verona.
Romeo ran straight to Friar Laurence's cell for refuge after he killed Tybalt, so he doesn't yet know his fate. Friar Laurence tells him, and persuades him that all is not lost. Only when the Nurse comes and talks about Juliet does he stop crying.

Banishment   *lines 12–70*

Verona was a walled town, with heavy gates guarding all the entrances from the outside world, making it difficult to escape notice on the way in or out. Both Romeo and Juliet are well aware of what banishment means: never to have the right and freedom to return to Verona. The idea of banishment terrifies them. They both see it as death.

The photograph above shows the walled town of Carcassone, in France. The only way in to the town was through the main gates, which were always guarded.

Work with a partner. Gather together all the definitions of banishment which Juliet says in Act 3 scene 2, and which Romeo says in Act 3 scene 3. For example, Juliet says being banished is like killing ten thousand Tybalts or like her father, her mother, Tybalt, Romeo, and herself, all dead.

Produce a diagram to show the idea of banishment as understood by Romeo and Juliet.

 ## Be merciful, say death   *lines 29–42*

Romeo cannot see that the Prince's sentence of banishment is better than a death sentence.

Work in groups of four or more. Read lines 29–42 by sentences, the rest of the group echoing all these words: 'here', 'Juliet', 'Romeo', 'he', 'her', 'she', 'I'. What kind of mood do his words show?

Then read the lines again, echoing a different group of words: 'banished', 'exile', 'death'.

Discuss your view of Romeo in these lines. Is he angry? Sad? Sorry for himself? Sorry for Juliet? Sorry for Tybalt? What does he want?

That name's cursed hand   *lines 101–107*

When the Nurse describes Juliet's despair and tears, Romeo focuses on the only thing he can think of which explains what has happened: his name. As he thinks his name must 'lodge' *in* him, he tries to destroy it and himself. He and Juliet have both had to accept that you cannot separate people from their names. You may have noticed that it is always Romeo's name, Montague, which is presented as the problem, not Juliet's.

Art thou a man?   *lines 108–133*

Friar Laurence is forced by Romeo's suicidal behaviour to argue him out of his despair. In lines 108–120 the Friar asks Romeo a series of questions, which he himself answers in lines 121–133.

Work with a partner. List the questions he asks Romeo, in a long column down the left side of your page. Discuss and note down what idea you think he is trying to put across to Romeo.

Then read lines 121–133. In the column on the right side of your page opposite the questions you have already listed, write down anything in these lines which you think is an answer. For example:

Questions	Answers
Art thou a man?	Thy noble shape is but a form of wax, Digressing from the valour of a man ...

There art thou happy   *lines 134–139*

Read lines 134–139. List the reasons the Friar gives Romeo for being 'happy'. Do you think he means 'happy' in the sense of cheerful, joyful? Is there another meaning to his words?

Does Romeo listen? *lines 108–144*

Work in groups of four or five. Your aim is to work out how
Romeo reacts to the Friar during these lines. The Friar starts off
very angry – he has just stopped Romeo from killing himself –
and then he has to find a way of proving to Romeo that things
could be worse.

Have one person as Romeo, the rest sharing out the Friar's lines.
Read slowly through the lines, giving yourselves time to discuss
with Romeo what actions *he* feels like doing at each of the Friar's
questions or statements, and what *you* think he should be doing.
Remember, the Friar is giving him a good telling-off, so many of
his words can be spoken with force: 'shame', 'perjury',
'misshapen', 'ignorance', and so on.

Friar Laurence's plan *lines 145–153*

Work with a partner. Use lines 145–153 and lines 166–170 to
work out what the Friar tells Romeo to do, and what he hopes to
do in the future. Discuss and note down any drawbacks you see
in his plan.

Act 3 scene 4

*Very late, Monday evening. Capulet's house, Verona.
Paris comes wooing Juliet the day after the feast. Both he and
Capulet completely ignore what Capulet said earlier about
Juliet's youth. While they are talking, the audience is aware
that Juliet is waiting for Romeo, or that they are already
together upstairs.*

Sir Paris

Paris has few words to say: how can you decide what kind of
person he is? A summary of his actions would be very short: on
Sunday afternoon he comes to Capulet's house to offer marriage
to Juliet; on Sunday evening he comes to the feast to look at
Juliet and other beautiful women; on Monday evening, very late,
he comes back to Capulet's house, to woo Juliet.

Look at his lines in Act 1 scene 2 lines 4–6 and 12, remind yourself of the feast scene Act 1 scene 5, and read lines 8–9, 18, and 29 in this scene.

Write entries in Paris's diary for each of these three occasions, adding in his thoughts. Include his reasons for wanting to marry Juliet, what he thought of her when he saw her at the feast, whether he danced with her (was he the knight Juliet was dancing with when Romeo first saw her?), and why he has taken no notice of what Capulet said about waiting two years.

Capulet   *lines 1–36*

Capulet talks in a very disjointed way in this scene. What is the matter with him?

In groups of five or six, read the whole scene, lines 1–36, changing reader at every punctuation mark. What did you notice about Capulet's lines?

Make a note of the lines spoken by Capulet which you think threaten danger or difficulties for Juliet in the future.

Act 3 scene 5

Very early Tuesday morning. Capulet's house, Verona.
At the beginning of the scene Juliet parts from Romeo. By the
end of it she is totally isolated from her parents and the Nurse,
and has only the Friar to turn to.

Wilt thou be gone?   *lines 1–36*

It is time for Romeo to leave for Mantua, but Juliet argues with him that it is not yet dawn.

Read lines 1–36 in pairs. The argument can be simply shown like this:

1   Juliet: It is not day.
2   Romeo: It is day.

3   Juliet: It is not day.
4   Romeo: It is day, but I'll stay and die.
5   Juliet: It is day.

Find the words spoken by Romeo and Juliet which match this outline.

Note down all the signs of day and night described by Romeo and Juliet in these lines.

Another way of tracking the development of their speech is to note down the *sounds* they talk of. The final sound Juliet speaks of threatens danger to Romeo. What is it?

Think'st thou we shall ever meet again? *lines 52–57*

Work with a partner. Read between you Romeo and Juliet's words in these lines. Discuss and write down your responses to these points:

- the play has so far led you to expect Juliet's words to come true
- the play has so far led you to expect Romeo's words to come true
- neither Romeo's nor Juliet's words in these lines are what you would expect them to say.

Do all these photos show Romeo and Juliet parting after their wedding night?

Evermore weeping   *lines 43–105*

Lady Capulet, on her husband's orders, has come to talk to
Juliet about the marriage with Paris. She finds Juliet weeping.

With a partner, read lines 43–70. At what point do you think
Juliet starts to cry? Lady Capulet assumes that she is crying for
the death of Tybalt, which only happened the previous
afternoon, but this hides the real reason for Juliet's tears.

Still with your partner, read lines 68–105 in parts, noticing as
you read where Juliet is speaking the truth.

A sudden day of joy   *lines 104–196*

Lady Capulet's announcement of the marriage comes as a
dreadful shock to Juliet. But to be true to Romeo, and to her
marriage vows, she will have to refuse to marry Paris.

Lead into your work on these lines by improvising a short scene
round this situation, working in groups of four: a rich father
wants his daughter to marry a wealthy young man; he has
arranged the day of the marriage without asking his daughter
first; her mother goes along with what the father says; the girl
refuses; the girl's nurse sticks up for her; the father loses his
temper and threatens to throw the girl out onto the streets.

Still in your groups of four, you are going to prepare a
performance of lines 104–196 to show the class. You will need to
think about:

■ Lady Capulet's attitude to Juliet – you will notice that it
   changes according to what Juliet and Capulet say
■ Capulet's attitude to Juliet – you will notice that it does not
   change. Think about his anger: suggest reasons why he
   becomes so enraged with Juliet
■ the Nurse – when she comes in at line 125 and sees Juliet
   weeping, what does she do? How does she react to Capulet's
   and Lady Capulet's words? What makes her speak at lines
   168–9 and 173?
■ Juliet – when does she go down on her knees? (She is
   kneeling by line 158.) Do her parents touch her, push her
   about, shout at her? Does she cry the whole time? Does she
   turn to the Nurse for support?

Which line from this scene would you use as a caption for this photograph?

I'll ne'er acknowledge thee   *lines 176–196*

Work with a partner. Read lines 176–196 and then note down:

■ Capulet's three main reasons for being so angry with Juliet
■ your views about his anger
■ whether you think his anger is justified.

Hot seat

Work as a class. Put two volunteers in the hot seat, as Capulet and Lady Capulet. Question them in turn very closely about their behaviour towards Juliet in this scene. Don't let them off lightly!

Some comfort, Nurse   *lines 213–226*

Work with a partner. Read lines 213–226. Is the Nurse talking sense? Can Juliet possibly agree with it? Make out two contrasting cases, one agreeing and one disagreeing with what the Nurse says. Copy the chart on page 55 and fill in the agree/disagree columns with your own words opposite each of the Nurse's statements. One has been done for you:

Nurse's statement	Agree	Disagree
Romeo is banished; all the world to nothing that he dares ne'er come back		
The County is a lovely gentleman	He's really handsome, rich, so well-mannered	No he isn't, she'd rather see a toad than him
Romeo's a dishclout to him		
This second match excels your first		
Your first is dead – or as good as		
You live here, with no use of him		

Discuss why the Nurse gives Juliet this advice. Has she suddenly realized the difficult position she is in for helping Juliet marry Romeo?

Act 4 scene 1

Tuesday afternoon. Friar Laurence's cell.
At the very place where she goes to seek help, Juliet meets the man who is the cause of her distress. The Friar's original good intentions are already disrupted, and he is forced to set Juliet off on a very dangerous course.

Paris   *lines 18–36*

This is the only opportunity Paris gets to woo Juliet. He speaks
directly to her, for the first time, about their marriage. Juliet is
forced to speak with double meanings, to avoid revealing her
true situation. Paris is trying to find out if Juliet loves him; she
keeps him at arm's length. Paris makes all the running: he asks
questions or makes statements, forcing Juliet to respond.

Work with a partner. Read lines 18–36 in parts, playing Paris as
very eager, friendly, and pleasant, and Juliet as very subdued,
defensive, and false. Decide whether this works. Vary the reading
until you feel you have got it right. Decide whether Juliet looks at
Paris, or keeps her head turned away. How rude can she afford
to be?

Discuss your opinion of Paris as a wooer. Are you impressed?
How does he compare with Romeo?

Discuss your view of Paris talking about Juliet as though he owns
her: 'Thy face is mine, and thou hast slander'd it'. What do you
think Juliet means in her reply: 'It may be so, for it is not mine
own'? Who does her face belong to?

Add another entry in Paris's diary, describing his meeting with
Juliet at Friar Laurence's cell. What has been his impression of
her?

With this knife   *lines 50–67*

Work with a partner. Suicide, which Juliet threatens at line 54,
and which Romeo has already threatened, was an act that any
man of the church would do all in his power to prevent. For
Elizabethans, suicide was a sin against God, and the souls of
suicides were eternally damned. Suicides could not be buried in
the consecrated ground of the church, and were often buried at
crossroads with a stake driven through them. Friar Laurence
must do all he can to prevent both Romeo and Juliet from taking
their own lives. If he fails, he knows what punishment their souls
will receive.

Read lines 50–67 between you. Pick out and write down the key words in each sentence, not more than four for each. What are Juliet's main concerns?

Discuss the Friar's reaction at line 54 when Juliet produces a knife, and at line 67 when she stops speaking: does he try to take it from her?

This distilled liquor drink thou off   *lines 93–106*

The Friar's description of Juliet's false death shows in advance what her real death later will be like.

Work with a partner. Read lines 93–106. Make out an entry for this potion, as it would appear in a chemist's book (pharmacopoeia). Use the headings 'Action', 'Symptoms', 'After-effects', 'Side effects', 'Not advised for –'.

Act 4 scene 2

Tuesday evening. Capulet's house.
Capulet, overjoyed with Juliet's new obedience, brings the marriage forward to Wednesday morning. Capulet cannot know that Juliet and 'this reverend holy friar' are planning to thwart him. When he says 'my heart is wondrous light' the audience knows that it won't be for long.

Henceforward I am ever rul'd by you   *lines 17–35*

Juliet's speech has become much more formal.

Work with a partner. Read all Juliet's words, lines 17–35, between you. Notice the words she uses: 'disobedient', 'opposition', 'behests', 'prostrate', 'henceforward', 'becomed', 'needful ornaments'. Discuss why she is talking like this.

Try reading her words again in two different ways, this time reading Capulet's lines also: first, make her sound very 'good' and obedient; then make her sound dead and unemotional.

Compare the two readings. Does either of them sound convincing?

My heart is wondrous light   *lines 16–32*

The last time Capulet spoke to Juliet, he was threatening to turn her out onto the street, and to disown her.

Work with a partner. Re-read his words to her in Act 3 scene 5 lines 176–196. Compare them with his words to her in this scene. What is your opinion of him as a father? What is your opinion of him as a person? Note down your ideas.

Act 4 scene 3

Tuesday night. Capulet's house.
In spite of her terror at what might go wrong, Juliet takes the potion. Her fear of waking before Romeo comes is the opposite of what finally happens. She does not consider that the Friar's plans for contacting Romeo in Mantua might go wrong.

Madam   *lines 7–11*

Juliet's words to her mother, like those to her father in the previous scene, are very formal and stilted. Note down the words that strike you as unusual for Juliet in lines 7–11. Why do you think she is talking like this to her mother?

My dismal scene   *lines 20–59*

Friar Laurence talked about the 'ancient vault where all the kindred of the Capulets lie' in Act 4 scene 1 lines 109–112. This vault or tomb would have been a large underground chamber, marked with a stone monument above ground, in which the dead Capulets were laid on stone biers. They were never actually buried in the ground. Juliet knows this, so can imagine the bones of these long-dead ancestors, lying on their biers or stacked on shelves, and has some idea of how a corpse rots in its shroud. Friar Laurence's plan could only work with burial arrangements like these.

This is claimed to be the vault of the Capulets, with one of the tombs. Can you see why Juliet would be frightened to be shut up in a tomb like this?

Juliet expresses her terror in long, incomplete sentences, asking herself questions for which she has no convincing answers.

Work with a partner. Read lines 20–59. Write down her answers to her first two questions:

■   what if it doesn't work?
■   what if it's a real poison?

Her third question (lines 30–32 – what if I wake before Romeo comes?) she answers at line 32, saying, 'There's a fearful point'. But this is not really an answer at all. It leads her into terrible imaginings. Match up her words with the statements below:

■   she'll be stifled
■   she'll run mad with fear
■   she'll be so terrified she'll kill herself.

Her idea of death, and what is in the tomb of the Capulets, is full of horror.

Hideous fears   *lines 33–57*

Work as a class. Read lines 33–57 round the class by punctuation marks. Repeat out loud each word about death, terror, blood, or decay as it is read.

Turn your reading into a frightening performance of these lines, by using your voices to whisper, make sound effects, shout, and even scream.

Act 4 scene 4

The early hours of Tuesday morning, 3 a.m. Capulet's house. The importance of this scene is to provide a time gap between Juliet's taking the potion and her being found 'dead'. It highlights the futility of Capulet's busy activity: the daughter he is doing this for is already 'dead'.

 ## Come, stir, stir, stir! *lines 1–27*

Work in groups of five. The scene is a very busy one. Read the whole scene, in parts. Note down what you learn about:

- preparations for the wedding feast
- the Nurse's name
- the customary time for weddings (roughly)
- what Capulet used to get up to
- what Lady Capulet feels about it
- logs – can you explain why they are needed in the middle of July? (Shakespeare may have included logs because the original story he based this play on was set in winter. You may also like to consider that although the play is set in Italy, much of the domestic detail seems to be English.)
- music for weddings
- where the bride and groom meet.

Put on a performance of this scene, making it as lively as possible. You will need to:

- take one part each
- read the scene through several times
- work out where people should come in and go out
- work out what people should do, where they should move
- decide what your own character is feeling. For example, Capulet seems to be very cheerful, Lady Capulet rather sharp; what about the Nurse and the servant?

Show your performance to the class.

Act 4 scene 5

Early Wednesday morning. Capulet's house.
This scene shows Juliet's 'death', and it gives space for a mourning ritual which would not be appropriate at the end of the play. Juliet's real death is mourned before it happens.

The kind of grief expressed in this scene is difficult for a modern audience to understand and sympathize with. It seems exaggerated and embarrassing. To people in other countries, where the public and ritualized expression of grief still occurs, this scene is perfectly acceptable.

The Nurse   *lines 1–16*

Work with a partner. Read lines 1–11. Which earlier appearance of the Nurse is this most like? Has she ever realized that Juliet cast her off?

Read lines 12–16. Share with your partner and then write down the thoughts that go through the Nurse's head, from when she says, 'What, dress'd!' (line 12).

O lamentable day!   *lines 17–32*

The Nurse and Juliet's parents lament Juliet's death privately.

Work in groups of three. Read lines 17–32, taking parts. Whisper the words, without hurrying. Read them again, trying to express through your voice the sense of shock felt by Juliet's family.

Select a statement from these lines which could be an epitaph for Juliet.

Death is my son-in-law   *lines 34–64*

Lady Capulet, the Nurse, Paris, and Capulet now each express their grief in a formal, public way, in comparison to the more private, family mourning earlier in the scene.

Work as a class. Read lines 34–64, changing over at punctuation marks, emphasizing the rhythm and speaking slowly and heavily.

Try other ways of making these lines work:
- play sad music in the background
- softly beat a drum in time to the rhythm of the words
- hum or sing quietly
- choose some of the words or lines as a chorus, to be spoken between other lines by a 'chorus' group.

Musicians, O musicians   *lines 96–140*

These are the musicians Paris brought with him for the wedding. Their words are connected with the mourning, but they provide a little light relief from the grieving.

Work in groups of four. Read lines 100–140, in parts. Use the outline below to help you with your understanding:

lines 96–105: they are all sad, Peter wants them to play a sad song.

lines 106–120: the first musician and Peter argue and threaten each other, because the musician won't play the tune Peter wants.

lines 121–133: Peter asks all the musicians a musical riddle; none of them gets it right.

lines 134–137: Peter gives them the answer, which is the words from a song.

lines 138–140: the musicians curse Peter, and stay for dinner.

Perform the little scene.

Imagine that you have been told the scene with the musicians must be cut from a production of the play. In a pair, one of you writes a convincing case for cutting it, the other writes a convincing case for keeping it. Use your arguments in a class discussion.

 ## The mourners: hotseating

Work as a whole class. Imagine that Capulet, Lady Capulet, the Nurse, and Paris all return to Capulet's house after the funeral of Juliet. They say little to each other, because they are all engrossed in their memories of Juliet, and in thinking of their behaviour towards her in the last few days.

Put volunteers in the hot seat as Capulet, Lady Capulet, the Nurse, and Paris, and ask them about Juliet and their relationship with her.

On your own, choose one of these characters: write down their thoughts.

Friar Laurence

The Friar's plan depends on him writing a letter to Romeo with all this news and with his instructions about what Romeo should do next. Write the letter, keeping it as brief as possible.

Act 5 scene 1

Wednesday afternoon. Mantua.
After being in Mantua for one day Romeo receives news of Juliet, but the wrong news from the wrong mouth. His reaction is an instant decision to go to Juliet's tomb and kill himself. He is determined to lie with her. He has no means of knowing that the information he has been given is false.

Her body sleeps in Capel's monument   *lines 17–23*

Balthasar, as a Montague servant, can only have seen Juliet's funeral at a distance. In spite of his promise earlier (Act 3 scene 3 lines 168–170), Friar Laurence has not found Balthasar to tell him of the change in Juliet's situation, or to give him letters for Romeo.

Then I defy you, stars!

Romeo's reaction is immediate and final: he knows exactly what he will do.

Before you work on the rest of this section, do this activity to highlight Romeo's change of attitude towards Fortune.

Stand in a circle as a whole class. You are only going to say a few words, so you have to make them work. First, round the group, say one after the other: 'O, I am Fortune's fool', starting very quietly but getting louder round the class. The last person make it a shout of misery. Try to pick up the cue very quickly, with no gap between one person and the next.

Second, do exactly the same with 'Then I defy you, stars', but add in a gesture as you say the words to show defiance to Fortune. All join in together on the last shout, with a huge noise and large gestures, so the stars will hear you! You should now have some idea of how Romeo feels.

Up to this point, Romeo has left his life in the hands of Fate, or the stars. Why is he *now* defying the stars?

Romeo's plan   *lines 25–34*

With a partner, read lines 25–34, and note down what Romeo intends to do before he dies.

Hast thou no letters to me from the Friar? *line 31*

Friar Laurence's promises for the future allowed Romeo to be cheerful and optimistic to Juliet when they parted. Look back at Act 3 scene 3 lines 148–153 and 168–170 for the Friar's words, and at Act 3 scene 5 lines 51–53 for what Romeo said to Juliet.

When you first heard Friar Laurence's promises, did you believe his words would come true? Write down the thoughts you had at that time.

Romeo now realizes his hopeful words cannot come true. Write down his thoughts about Juliet and her unexpected death, and the end of all his hopes.

A caitiff wretch

Romeo has resolved to kill himself to lie with Juliet in the tomb. He needs a 'mortal drug', the sale of which is illegal. What makes him think the apothecary will sell it to him?

Work with a partner. Read lines 35–54 between you. Make a list of all the evidence about the apothecary that helped Romeo conclude: 'Here lives a caitiff wretch would sell it him'.

The apothecary is extremely poor, yet he is unwilling to sell this poison. Read lines 68–75 between you. Discuss and then write down your answers to these questions:

■ Which of Romeo's lines would have been most persuasive?
■ What does Romeo say in these lines which is a comment on himself?
■ Has Romeo changed since the beginning of the play?

Act 5 scene 2

Wednesday night. Friar Laurence's cell, Verona.
This short scene contains the most crucial piece of information. Friar Laurence's letter to Romeo has never even left Verona. It is now impossible for him to have Romeo at Juliet's side when she awakes.

Going to find a bare-foot brother

Friar John's explanation for his failure to leave Verona is regarded by many commentators as a real weakness in the plot of *Romeo and Juliet*.

With a partner, read lines 5–12. Work out what happened to delay him. These questions will help you:
■ Who was he looking for?
■ Why?
■ Where did he look?
■ What was this person doing?
■ Where did he find him?
■ What happened to them?
■ What happened to the letter?

Do you find this story convincing?

Make up an argument in support of this piece of plotting, emphasizing that Friar John's story is quite acceptable.

Make up an opposing argument, explaining what is wrong with it.

Join up with another pair, listen to their two arguments, give your own arguments, and decide which arguments you found the most convincing.

Romeo hath had no notice

Work in groups of three or four. The Friar doesn't know that Romeo has had news. Romeo doesn't know that the news was inaccurate.

Take some time at this stage to look at what each character in the play now knows or thinks about Romeo and Juliet. Write what characters know and think in a list, and add the words 'right' or 'wrong' by each item. To start you off:

Romeo	thinks Juliet is dead	wrong
Friar Laurence	knows Juliet is not dead	right
	thinks Romeo is in Mantua	wrong

Do the same for the following characters: Capulet, Lady Capulet, the Nurse, the Prince, Benvolio.

Does anyone know everything, apart from the audience?

Act 5 scene 3

Wednesday night. The churchyard, Verona.
In this last scene of the play, all must be explained and resolved. The Friar's plan goes completely astray; Paris, Tybalt, Romeo, and Juliet all lie dead in the same tomb; but at last the two households are shamed into making peace.

Do not interrupt me in my course   *lines 22–39*

Work in groups of four or five. Romeo's decisiveness is almost aggressive. His behaviour makes Balthasar suspicious; even in Mantua Balthasar suspected what Romeo was up to.

Using lines 22–39 and what Romeo said to him in Act 5 scene 1 lines 25–33, write down Balthasar's account of this event in his life.

I will apprehend him   *lines 49–57*

Romeo and Paris have not met in the play. Paris recognizes Romeo, but Romeo does not know who is confronting him until it is too late.

Read lines 49–57. Does Paris suggest here his reasons for disliking Romeo? Quickly note down all the insulting words he speaks about Romeo.

 ## Tempt not a desperate man   *lines 54–67*

Work in groups of three. Romeo's response to Paris's words echoes his response to Tybalt earlier, in the same way that Paris's words echo Tybalt's.

One person read Paris's lines 54–57. Two people read Romeo's lines 58–67, in sentences, changing over at each full stop. Work on ways of bringing out the contrast between the two speeches: Paris very aggressive, Romeo pleading.

Romeo calls himself 'a desperate man'. What is he desperate to avoid? What is he desperate to do?

 ## A grave? O no, a lantern   *lines 84–120*

Work in groups of up to eight. Romeo's words are his farewell to the world. Use the speech divisions below to work out who he is talking to:

lines 84–87:	A grave? . . . interr'd,
lines 88–91:	How oft . . . a lightning?
lines 91–96:	O my love . . . advanced there.
lines 97–101:	Tybalt . . . forgive me, cousin!
lines 101–112:	Ah, dear Juliet . . . flesh.
lines 112–115:	Eyes . . . death!
lines 116–119:	Come . . . my love!
lines 119–120:	O true . . . quick.
line 120:	Thus with a kiss I die.

Give each reader in the group one set of lines, as shown above. Practise your lines until you are satisfied with your reading, and then put them all together. Your aim is to make clear Romeo's state of mind.

Romeo says at line 88:

> How oft when men are at the point of death
> Have they been merry! which their keepers call
> A lightning before death.

Do you think that Romeo dies happy? Still in pairs, discuss your response and note down your ideas.

O much I fear some ill unthrifty thing   *lines 121–146*

Friar Laurence arrives at the tomb to be by Juliet's side when she wakes. He has no idea of what he will find.

Work with a partner. Read lines 121–146 in parts. Decide at what line Friar Laurence begins to fear that all is not as it should be. Decide how Balthasar would speak his lines – is he frightened? Does his fear start to infect Friar Laurence?

Let me die   *lines 161–169*

When Juliet kisses Romeo, what does she realize? She has no time to do anything except react to the noises and voices she can hear around her. How do you think she should say, 'Thy lips are warm!'? Does she cry?

Whoe'er you find, attach   *lines 171–180*

The Watch, who have been roused by Paris's page, turn these private deaths into a public tragedy: they order the Prince, the Capulets, and the Montagues to be woken up and brought to the tomb. They also order anyone found in the churchyard or nearby to be arrested. There is as yet no clear explanation of what has happened, for them. The audience knows.

Inquest into the deaths of Romeo, Juliet, and Paris
lines 230–265

The Friar tells of his part in the lives of these young people. His story is added to by what Balthasar knows, by the letter Romeo wrote for his father, and by the page's evidence.

Read the Friar's lines 230–265. Regard them as evidence in a court of law. Working as a class, set up an inquest into these deaths, in which the Friar, Balthasar, Paris's page, the Capulets, the Montagues, the Nurse, and Benvolio are all questioned. Members of the class take on the parts of these characters, and you should also have a coroner to chair the inquest. The rest of the class questions the witnesses. Keep a note of the answers given by witnesses, and if you are not satisfied, ask them further questions.

Write up the proceedings of the coroner's inquest into these deaths, to be reported in the *Verona Times*.

All are punished

Work on your own or with a partner. The civil strife in Verona has spread its net wide. It has caught all the young people in its mesh, except Benvolio: Mercutio, Tybalt, Paris, Romeo, and Juliet are all dead. Now the older generation are feeling its effects: Lady Montague 'is dead tonight. Grief of [Romeo's] exile hath stopp'd her breath'. Lady Capulet says, 'This sight of death is as a bell, that warns my old age to a sepulchre.' And Friar Laurence speaks of his 'short date of breath', and says, 'Let my old life be sacrific'd, some hour before his time'.

Write down your thoughts and feelings about the fate of the young people, including your thoughts about how much blame you attach to the adults.

Poor sacrifices of our enmity! *lines 295–303*

Work with a partner. Read lines 295–303. What is your opinion of this gesture from these two fathers? How would you commemorate the deaths of these young people?

Write epitaphs for Romeo and Juliet, to be inscribed on the base of their golden statues. An epitaph is an inscription on a gravestone or a monument, usually quite short, which gives brief details about the life and death of the dead person. Sometimes other words are added to sum up something special about the dead person. Think about anything special you would want to say about Romeo and Juliet.

 ## A glooming peace *lines 304–309*

Work as a whole class. To experience a fitting ending to the play, try this final assignment.

The class divides into six groups, and each group takes one of the lines. The groups have two things to do:
- make up a freeze frame which illustrates your line
- work out a way of saying your line, either in unison, using repetition, or echoing, or other sounds, and decide on the tone of voice you will use.

When each group is ready, take up position round the room in your freeze frame, and speak your line as you have practised it.

If possible, add in the sound of a tolling bell, or gently bang a deep drum.

Practise this until you feel you have achieved a worthy end activity for the play.

Overview

Characters

Character profiles

These character profiles can be used for revision, or for introducing characters before the play is studied.

Prince Escalus

You are the ruler of Verona, an Italian city like a very small country in its own right. Verona has a high city wall all round it, so you can control who comes in and who goes out through the big city gates. You have not managed to control the feud that has been going on between the Capulets and the Montagues, or perhaps you did not try. The street fight on Sunday morning is the third time the two families have caused a public brawl, involving many other people. On this occasion, however, you lose your patience, and threaten death to anybody found fighting in the streets in the future. You make Capulet and Montague come to you separately to talk about this latest violence. Capulet says afterwards that he feels he and Montague should be able to keep the peace from now on. Two of your kinsmen are involved in the events of the play: Count Paris, who wants to marry Juliet, and Mercutio, who is a friend of Romeo.

Paris

You are a wealthy young relative of Prince Escalus, the ruler of Verona. Your title is Count or County Paris. You want to marry Juliet Capulet, and you are quite persistent in your attempts to get her father to agree to the marriage. At first he puts you off, as he would prefer you to wait for two years, but later he agrees to let you marry Juliet in a few days' time. You are good-looking, and probably want a wife in the same way that Capulet wanted a wife – not particularly for love, but more for the purpose of having children who can inherit your wealth. Later events show that you did feel much affection for Juliet.

Mercutio

You are a relation of the Prince, and a friend of Romeo and Benvolio. You much prefer Romeo when he is not miserably in love. You do not show any interest in love yourself. You enjoy teasing women, and are almost insulting to Juliet's nurse when you meet her on Monday morning. You also enjoy teasing Romeo, particularly about his love for Rosaline. You are witty, and enjoy amusing and sometimes sexually suggestive word-play. You encourage Romeo to go to the Capulet feast, against his own better judgement, but you do not witness his meeting with Juliet, and know nothing about his love for her. You are not involved in the Capulet/Montague feud, but your own quick-tempered nature makes you very volatile. Your dislike of Tybalt, and the way he uses a sword, makes it impossible for you to walk away from a fight with him.

Montague

As head of the Montague household, you are half-responsible for the feud that has existed between your two families for years. You have made no effort to stop it, and do not appear to know that your own servants are quite happy to keep it going. You make every effort to join in the fighting in the street on Sunday morning, but your wife holds you back. You are the father of Romeo, but your contact with him is so slight that you do not know where he is on that Sunday morning, nor do you know what is the matter with him. You never meet him during the play, and have no idea what he has been doing. Your nephew Benvolio keeps you informed as far as he can, and he and Mercutio feel free to come and go to your house, and to dine there.

Lady Montague

You are Romeo's mother, but share with your husband an ignorance of his life and affairs. You seem to think the feud with the Capulets is pointless; you certainly prevent your husband from joining in the fighting by physically holding him back. In spite of not knowing where Romeo is on Sunday morning, you are certainly very concerned about him, and are very pleased he was not involved in the brawl.

Romeo

You are the only son of the Montague household. You are about eighteen and don't see very much of your parents. At the moment you are desperately 'in love' with a woman called Rosaline, who wants nothing to do with you. This makes you so unhappy that you wander alone at night in the wood outside Verona, and the minute the sun begins to rise you come home and lock yourself in your room with the curtains drawn and the shutters closed. When you see the results of the street fight, you are dismayed. You have been brought up in a family that is feuding with another, so you know that in Verona, who you are matters more than what you are. You know some members of the Capulet family, but you do not know Juliet.

Benvolio

You are a nephew of Romeo's father, Montague, so you are in fact Romeo's cousin. You and Romeo are friends, and you are very supportive of him. You are a peaceful person: you try to stop the street fight although Tybalt threatens to kill you and you have to defend yourself. The Prince asks you for an account of how the fight started, and you tell Romeo's parents where he is on that Sunday morning. You are fed up with Romeo being in love with Rosaline, because, as you quite rightly point out to him, he has never compared her with anyone else. When an opportunity arises for Romeo to see other young women as well as Rosaline at Capulet's feast, you get him to go with you, masked.

Capulet

You are the head of the Capulet household, and have continued the feud which you started against the Montagues years ago, although no one can remember what the original reason for it was. You try to join in the street fight on Sunday morning, although your wife scorns your efforts and tries to stop you getting hold of a sword. Two servants from your own household provoked this fight, but you make no effort to control them. You are a respected member of Veronese society, and invite many rich and powerful people to your feast. Your daughter Juliet is your only child, and you still want to protect her – you are not going to push her into marrying Paris, who has come asking for her hand in marriage, but you would rather let her wait for two years. Your wife controls you from time to time, as you are very quick-tempered and likely to do rash things. You are quite old compared to your wife, about fifty-five.

Lady Capulet

You have borne Capulet several children, and had Juliet when you were about fourteen. You are probably about twenty-nine. You don't show much affection towards your daughter, leaving that side of things to the Nurse who has always looked after her. You think your husband is a bit of an old fool, and you prevent him from joining in the street fight on Sunday morning. You also suspect that he may not always have been faithful to you; he certainly chased after other women when he was younger. You talk to Juliet about the possibility of marriage to Paris, but not really in terms of love, more in terms of a business proposition. However, you are not pushing her into marriage yet, simply asking her to think about Paris and to look at him at the Capulet feast. You are very fond of your nephew Tybalt. You and your husband sometimes travel to other places. When Juliet was three you went to Mantua.

Juliet

You are the only surviving child of the Capulet household, and until now you have been very protected. In two weeks' time, on 31 July, you will be fourteen. Your father has been asked for your hand in marriage by Paris, a rich nobleman related to the Prince of Verona. Your mother asks you whether you would like to get married, but you have no idea whether you would like to or not. However, you are prepared to look at Paris and decide what you think of him, at the Capulet feast being held on Sunday evening. You are still an innocent girl; you have not been out into the world. You have a nurse who has been part of your household since you were born, and who is more important to you than your mother. You would tell her things you would not tell your mother.

Tybalt

You are Lady Capulet's nephew, and therefore Capulet's nephew by marriage. You hate all Montagues, and when you see fighting going on in the street between Capulet and Montague servants you join in. Rather than stop the fighting, you threaten death to Benvolio, the one person who is trying to stop it. You do not appear to be interested in getting married. You are about the same age as Romeo. You are a very skilled swordsman and know all the right technical terms for passes and thrusts with the sword, as well as all the other formal movements which are part of swordsmanship. You are extremely hot-tempered, although you can be controlled by your uncle Capulet. Fighting seems to be an important part of your life. You know your enemies, the Montagues, so well, that you can recognize them by their voices even when you cannot see their faces.

Nurse

You have been with the Capulet household for about fourteen years, since Juliet was born. Your husband died some years ago, and your own child, Susan, born at the same time as Juliet, also died, probably as a baby. You were Juliet's wet-nurse – you breast-fed her – and have cared very lovingly for her ever since. You have lost most of your teeth. (You have only four left!) You are usually a cheerful person. You are very keen for Juliet to get married, and you enjoy making jokes and suggestive remarks about sex. You don't see yourself as a very clever person, but you will stand up for what you think is right, although sometimes you let your principles give way to convenience, which you would call good sense. You are much closer to Juliet than her mother is. Lady Capulet is prepared to listen your opinions.

Friar Laurence

You are a Franciscan friar in the monastery of Verona. You are, therefore, a Roman Catholic, as are all the other people in this play. People come to you to confess their sins and to be forgiven (they call it going to shrift, to be shriven) in the name of God. You are respected and important in the community. You have great skills with plants and herbs, and know which parts of them can be used for good, and which for bad purposes. You live very much in tune with nature. You are very important to Romeo as his father confessor. He tells you everything that's on his mind, even when he doesn't tell his friends. You know all about his love for Rosaline, and have often advised him to forget her, thinking that what he felt for her was not true love but infatuation (you call it 'doting'). You've listened to Romeo groaning, sighing and crying for Rosaline, so you are quite used to his emotional nature. Juliet also comes to you for confession, but you know nothing about their first meeting until after it has happened.

These profiles show the main characters as they are near the beginning of the play. The 'Profiles' work below can be done before work is started on the play, to help you become familiar with the characters very quickly. The 'Final profiles' work is intended to be done after you have worked on the play.

Profiles

Before you start work on the play, divide into groups of six. Allocate two of the character profiles to each person in the group. (It may help to make copies of them on separate sheets first.) Count Montague and Lady Montague as one profile. You each now read and 'learn' your characters.

Take the part of each of your characters, and in turn, tell the group about yourself from what you have read in the profile. Start off like this: 'My name is . . . and I am . . . ' Try not to look at your character profiles once the group has started the telling.

In your group, you may ask characters questions about themselves when they have finished talking. If you cannot answer a questions, say, 'I don't know yet,' and make a note of the question.

Final profiles

When you have finished work on the play, write the rest of your characters' descriptions to include everything else which happens to them. Work in your original groups, and finish telling your group about your characters. Even those who die should do this, and speak about themselves from beyond the grave! The group can ask questions about you as before.

Minor characters 1: dramatic importance

Many of the characters only play small parts, yet they are still very important. Working with a partner, copy and complete the grid on page 77 to show the dramatic importance of the minor characters. You are aiming to show what they do in the play, and to prove that it matters.

Name of character	What they do, when	Why it is important
Abram	Fights Sampson and Gregory, Act 1 scene 1	It starts off the feud again and leads to the Prince's threat.
Lady Montague	Worries about Romeo, Act 1 scene 1	It lets us know that he has a caring mother.
	Dies, Act 5 scene 3	It shows us her grief for her son.

Minor characters 2: point of view

Several minor characters only see a very limited part of the action, so they might not know about the final outcome. For example, Sampson and Gregory, as members of the Capulet household, are likely to hear what happened at the end, but how much do you think the Apothecary knows?

On your own, choose one of the minor characters and make up an account of the events of the play in which they are involved, from their point of view.

Interviews for a local paper

You can then join with a partner, and each interview the other, in role, for a report in the local Verona evening paper, to be called 'Tragic deaths of top Verona young – on the spot reports'.

In your interviews, try to get characters to say not only what they know, but what they *feel* about what happened, and whether they think they bear any responsibility for any of the events.

Statement game

Listed below are statements about ten of the main characters in *Romeo and Juliet*. In groups, take one or more of the statements, and:

- decide whether you agree or disagree with the statement
- find evidence (quotations from the play or reference to parts of the play) to back up your opinion
- share your work with the rest of the class.

You can take this one stage further by allowing the class to question each group about its opinions, and to challenge them to further justify what they have said.

Statements

1 The Prince bears no responsibility for what happens in the play.

2 Tybalt is largely to blame for the feud breaking out again.

3 Romeo was only in love with Juliet because she loved him; he would have loved Rosaline just as much if she'd returned his love.

4 Capulet does not really care about Juliet; he treats her like something to be sold.

5 The Nurse acted very responsibly towards Juliet and her parents.

6 Juliet behaved thoughtlessly and recklessly, with no consideration for anyone except herself.

7 Mercutio was to blame for his own death.

8 Paris would have been a much more suitable husband for Juliet than Romeo.

9 Friar Laurence should not have been forgiven by the Prince for what he did.

10 Benvolio does nothing useful in this play; he may as well not be in it.

Character jigsaw

Many people in the play are very complicated and show more than one side to their character. It is difficult to pin them down and say precisely what they are like. Work with a partner or on your own to make up character jigsaws for some of the main characters: write into drawn jigsaw pieces one aspect of your chosen character, and add in the line reference from the play as evidence for your statement. Use the example below to start you off:

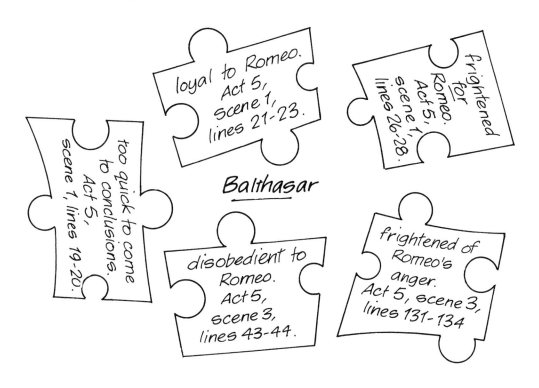

loyal to Romeo.
Act 5,
scene 1,
lines 21-23.

frightened for Romeo. Act 5, scene 1, lines 26-28.

too quick to come to conclusions. Act 5, scene 1, lines 19-20.

Balthasar

disobedient to Romeo. Act 5, scene 3, lines 43-44.

frightened of Romeo's anger. Act 5, scene 3, lines 131-134

Freeze frames

You were invited to produce several freeze frames as you worked through the play. You can now use this technique again to good effect to work out more about the relationships between characters, and to test yourselves on how well you know the play.

Work in groups of either two or three. Choose two or three characters to work on, and work out three freeze frames to show their relationship at different moments in the play. For example, to show the relationship betwen Juliet and Lady Capulet, you could choose these three moments:

1   when Lady Capulet is encouraging Juliet to marry Paris
2   when Lady Capulet says to Juliet, 'Do as thou wilt, for I have done with thee' (Act 3 scene 5 line 204)

3 Lady Capulet weeping over the 'dead' Juliet in Act 4 scene 5 or weeping over the dead Juliet in Act 5 scene 3.

Show your freeze frames to the class, who do two things:
- guess which characters and which moments in their relationship are being shown
- question each character in the freeze frame about their thoughts at that precise moment.

Inquest

At the end of the play, the Prince says, 'Some shall be pardoned, and some punished'. All the young people, apart from Benvolio, are dead. In the two families there is no one left to carry on the family name, and there will be no more children.

The Prince sets up an inquest into the five deaths, at which all those involved are required to give evidence, including the Prince himself. The characters required to give evidence are:

Capulet
Lady Capulet
Montague
Benvolio
the Nurse
Friar Laurence
the Prince.

To prepare for the inquest, divide the class into fourteen groups:

- seven groups (with maybe two or three people in each) to each work on the defence of one of the characters. One of your group takes on the role of your character during the inquest. The rest of the group will speak in their defence. Make sure your character can answer questions about all the dead people they were associated with, and that they can make themselves appear as innocent as possible

- seven groups (with two or three people in each) to each work on the prosecution of one of the characters. Try to come up with questions which will force your character to admit their guilt.

You will also need a coroner, who could be your teacher, to be in charge of the proceedings. The characters should be questioned by their prosecuting groups, and should defend themselves as well as possible with the help of their defence group.

During each character's session in the witness box, the coroner can allow questions to be put to the character by the rest of the class, who can also act as the jury, but at the end of each witness session the coroner must come to a verdict, and pass a recommendation for punishment or forgiveness.

Plot

Bare bones

The aim of a bare bones presentation is to strip the play down to its bare essentials, and then spend no more than about five minutes showing the whole play. As there are twenty-four scenes in *Romeo and Juliet*, a good way to do this work is to divide the scenes up into manageable sections. Have six groups of people, working on four scenes each.

In your group, select out from your scenes no more than four key moments. Note them down, and add the lines spoken at the key moments and the characters who speak them. Rehearse your key moments, having members of your group to act the different characters. If possible, learn your lines!

The whole class then comes together to act out these bare bones scenes in sequence. Try to present the whole of *Romeo and Juliet* in five minutes!

Director's notes

Work in groups of about four for this. Imagine you have been asked to help direct a production of *Romeo and Juliet*. Before rehearsals start you have to help make decisions about all the aspects of a stage performance.

Below is a preliminary set of director's notes, more like a list of possible ideas, to get you going. At this stage no decisions have been reached. Your task is to make definite recommendations in response to these ideas, and to produce a set of clear, labelled pre-production notes including sketches for the director which he or she can put into action during rehearsals and which he or she can use in discussions with the stage crew and production teams.

A hint: the first big decision to be made is usually about when the production is to be set. This affects all the other decisions.

Romeo and Juliet- production dates June/July
Aimed at mainly young audience — 14-20

Preliminary notes
Period and setting - modern? If so, where?
              Why? - Bring out relevance, etc.
       Period? - If so, when? — Shakespearean?
                              Other?
                              Italian, 13th century?
   Why? What's the point?
   If modern - does language fit?

Costumes - depend on above, but how many can we
     afford? Can we have any costume changes?
            R and J for wedding?
                  for farewell scene? - they've just
        spent night together - night clothes?

Set, staging - depends on period - how elaborate?
          - just suggest everything? - minimal set? Must
          we have a balcony?
          - or more definite - have to bear in mind all the
          different settings - Juliet's house
                               the street
                               the monument
                               Mantua

You may choose to do this activity for the whole play, which is a very big undertaking, or you may choose one scene or act of the play to focus on.

Display your finished notes and sketches for other groups to see, and compare suggestions each group has made.

Sound and music – music needed: feast scene/dancing
Friar Laurence's cell – wedding?
at end?
Musicians' scene – is it in?
Bell for funerals?
Clocks to indicate time passing?

Fights – use as many people as poss.
Need swords and daggers – fight director?
Lot of rehearsal needed here – can't risk accidents.

Props – apart from swords? Any? Paris has flowers at end, all those mattocks, bars of iron, lanterns, etc.
Can't think of anything else.

Lighting – real problem – most of play at night – is it? Need to think out use of spotlights maybe, or really use the lanterns somehow.

Casting

Casting a play presents challenges to a director, often because there is only a limited budget, and the number of actors has to be kept to a minimum.

How a director casts a production may also depend on what staging decisions have been made.

Imagine that you are being asked to cast a production of *Romeo and Juliet*: you have already done the 'Director's notes' activity, and you know what kind of production you are aiming for. Work in the same group if possible, and make your casting recommendations for a full-scale production of the play.

You will need to bear in mind:

- age of characters – what is the evidence from the play? Do actors need to fit this?

- appearance of characters – any evidence from the play?

- number of characters – any doubling-up possible? Could Tybalt play the Apothecary, for example? Do all minor characters need a separate actor?

- crowd scenes – which are the crowd scenes? How can they be made to look like crowd scenes with the minimum number of actors?

You can cast the play in a general way, for example by stating that the actor to play Capulet should be about fifty years old and be made up to look his own age, *or* you can recommend casting actors you have seen on TV, on film, or in the theatre.

Produce a clearly set-out list of recommendations for casting the play, which takes account of the considerations listed above.

Compare your work with another group's, or come together as a class and discuss all the problems you came across.

Look at the photographs on the opposite page. Would you cast any of these as Juliet?

Language and verse

Language of the play

You will already have worked out and understood the simple words in the play which are unfamiliar at first:

yea – yes
nay – no
hath – has
ere – before

and the way words are shortened to fit the length of the verse line – 'over' becomes 'o'er', 'it is' becomes ''tis'.

You will also have had to become familiar with the way characters call each other 'thou' instead of 'you', and you may already have worked out that when you say 'thou' you have to change the verb ending: 'thou speakest', for example.

Do some research on the use of 'thou' in the play. Working with a partner, produce a set of explanations about when this word is used between characters, and what it shows about their relationship. Use examples from the play to support what you are saying. Compare your findings with the class.

Verse

This work on verse can be done in pairs or as a whole class. The two main ideas to grasp about verse, and about the way this play was written, are *rhyme* and *rhythm*. Rhyme is quite easy: all kinds of nursery rhymes and children's songs and game chants rhyme, as you will remember. Rhyme patterns are also easily recognized. Rhythm can be more complex: practise beating out the rhythm in the lines printed below, and also try your hand at other lines from the play.

Rhythm

The main verse form in *Romeo and Juliet*, as in all Shakespeare's plays, is 'blank verse', or to give it its more formal label, 'iambic pentameter'. This was a very common and conventional way of writing plays during the sixteenth and seventeenth centuries, and most dramatists seem to have preferred it. The iambic pentameter is a five-beat line usually of ten syllables (sometimes an eleventh creeps in) in which the stresses alternate, as in this example:

> But sóft! What líght through yónder wíndow bréaks?
> It ís the éast, and Júliet ís the sún!

(Stresses are marked with the symbol ⁄ above the syllable to be stressed.)

As you read the lines aloud, beat out the stresses to get the feel of the rhythm.

Blank verse doesn't rhyme. Even so, it is a stylized way of writing, which is still flexible enough to give the illusion of being very close to ordinary speech.

Rhyme

At some points in the play characters speak in a rhyming form of iambic pentameter:

> Did mý heart lóve till nów? Forswéar it, síght!
> For Í ne'er sáw true béauty tíll this níght.

This kind of two-line rhyme is called a 'couplet'. However, it is worth remembering that couplets can be in any line length and rhythm – the label simply means two lines (a couplet) which rhyme.

The speech of many of the characters is neither consistently rhymed nor unrhymed verse but alternates between the two, often in the same speech as in this example:

> At this same ancient feast of Capulet's
> Sups the fair Rosaline, whom thou so loves,
> With all the admired beauties of Verona.
> Go thither; and, with unattainted eye
> Compare her face with some that I shall show,
> And I will make thee think thy swan a crow.
> (Act 1 scene 2 lines 82–87)

Benvolio moves out of blank verse into a couplet to round off what he is saying, and to give it vocal impact. Often, the last speaker in a scene has a couplet for the last two lines he or she speaks, to indicate that one piece of action has come to an end.

Other characters speak entire speeches in couplets (for example Capulet describing his 'old accustomed feast' to Paris, Act 1 scene 2 lines 13–33).

Although they have both already spoken in rhymed verse, when Romeo and Juliet meet and talk in the balcony scene (Act 2 scene 2) they speak entirely in unrhymed blank verse, apart from a closing couplet.

You may like to try to work out what effect this switching between rhymed and unrhymed verse has:

1   Can you work out any pattern to it?
2   Do some characters always speak one way or always the other?
3   Do different situations in the play seem to call for one form rather than the other?
4   Would rhyming always be appropriate?
5   Would unrhymed verse always be appropriate?

Formal rhymed verse

On four occasions in the play the sonnet form is used: it is as if the situation requires a more formal and rigid verse form. A sonnet is a fourteen-line verse, always concluding with a couplet, in which the first lines set out a situation, problem or statement, and the last lines attempt to resolve it. Sonnet writing was the height of fashion in Shakespeare's day for educated young men, who wrote sonnet sequences about love. Shakespeare wrote his own sonnet sequence, 154 sonnets in all!

Two of the sonnets, which are not so easy to spot, are in Act 1 scene 2 when Lady Capulet describes Paris to Juliet in a sonnet, and in Act 1 scene 5 when Romeo and Juliet meet at the Capulet feast. You can perhaps see this second sonnet as a symbol of the coming together of the two young lovers into one unit.

Can you find the other two sonnets?

Who speaks prose?

You will have noticed that some characters never speak in blank verse, only in prose, while other characters sometimes speak in blank verse and sometimes in prose. The Nurse is a good example here. Look back over her lines and make a note of where she speaks in blank verse and where she speaks in prose. Can you come up with any explanation for this?

Look back over the play and find your own examples of:

- unrhymed blank verse
- rhymed verse or couplets
- a speech containing both rhymed and unrhymed verse
- prose.

Either copy them out or note down the line references. Add any conclusions you have reached about the use of verse and prose in the play.

Get the rhythm

Try your hand at working out the line divisions in this extract from the Prince's speech, in Act 1 scene 1 of the play, which has been printed with no punctuation as a piece of prose. Copy it out and mark in the lines, or copy it out into lines as you go along. Then try to put in the missing punctuation. Compare your efforts with the real thing.

> Rebellious subjects enemies to peace profaners of this neighbour-stained steel will they not hear what ho you men you beasts that quench the fire of your pernicious rage with purple fountains issuing from your veins on pain of torture from those bloody hands throw your mistemper'd weapons to the ground and hear the sentence of your moved prince three civil brawls bred of an airy word by thee old Capulet and Montague have thrice disturb'd the quiet of our streets and made Verona's ancient citizens cast by their grave beseeming ornaments to wield old partisans in hands as old canker'd with peace to part your canker'd hate if ever you disturb our streets again your lives shall pay the forfeit of the peace for this time all the rest depart away you Capulet shall go along with me and Montague come you this afternoon to know our further pleasure in this case to old Freetown our common judgement-place once more on pain of death all men depart

To really 'get the rhythm', try talking to your partner in blank verse: remember to go for ten syllables and five beats. Here are some examples to set you on your way:

1   This is the saddest play that I have read
2   I wish the Prince had stopped the feud before
3   The lovers never really had a chance
4   If I go on like this I'll start to cry

Themes and ideas

Violence

Actual and threatened violence runs through *Romeo and Juliet*, from the first fighting in Act 1 scene 1 to Juliet's stabbing herself in Act 5 scene 3. The love between Juliet and Romeo is shaped by the violent events which surround it.

To give you an understanding of how much violence there is in the play, work in five groups, taking one act each. You are looking for lines and evidence to complete a chart like the one below.

Act 1 scene 1		
Character and line ref.	*Actual*	*Threatened*
Sampson and Gregory lines 1 – 60	Attack and provoke Abram	Say what they'll do to Montague men and maids
Capulet line 73	————	Asks for his sword
Montague line 77	————	Tries to get free of Lady Montague
Prince lines 94 – 100	————	Death sentence on anyone who fights
Tybalt lines 63 – 69	Fights Benvolio and taunts him – 'coward'	Hates all Montagues. Threatens Benvolio with death

Within each group, divide your act between you and work through your sections individually, so that you complete your searches as efficiently as possible.

As you work through the play, you'll notice how characters also *describe* or *threaten* violent actions or events, which may never happen. Include these in your chart.

Collect the finished charts together, either as a wall display which the class can look at, or as a reference book called 'Violence in *Romeo and Juliet*'.

Love

There are several different kinds of love in the play, but the play directs our attention to the romantic passion between Romeo and Juliet. Although their love is destroyed by the violence around it, it is powerful and passionate. Both Romeo and Juliet frequently express ideas about love, and show their love for each other through their words and images.

Work with a partner for this activity.

Romeo

Look at Romeo and his words first: remember that he loved Rosaline before he met Juliet, so he has a different set of experiences from Juliet. Pick out about eight of the lines or groups of lines Romeo speaks about love, to represent his feelings from the beginning of the play through to the end where he kills himself for love.

Juliet

Juliet only loves once, and then only for four days, but her love is intense and her loyalty to Romeo unshakeable. Pick out about eight of her lines or groups of lines, to represent the depth and strength of her love for Romeo.

Collect together your sixteen quotations. Your aim is to find a suitable way of presenting your selection. You might decide to present your quotations in a small booklet, with suitable illustrations, or as a wall display or poster, or as a series of storyboards.

Whatever you choose, show your finished work to the class and discuss the different choices of each group.

Oxymorons

Conflict and love are opposites. Because the love of Romeo and Juliet is set in the middle of conflict, the thoughts and language of the play have to express and come to terms with these opposites.

When Romeo sees the results of the first street brawl, his immediate reaction is to say, 'Here's much to do with hate, but more with love'. He then tries to find a way of linking love and hate in single thoughts. He comes up with 'brawling love', 'loving hate', 'heavy lightness', and 'still-waking sleep'. These opposite ideas linked together in this way are called oxymorons.

Both Romeo and Juliet use oxymorons at certain moments of the play, often when they are faced with situations they cannot cope with.

Working with a partner, look back at the words spoken by Romeo and Juliet and produce a list of the oxymorons they speak.

Select out two oxymorons from your list and develop them into poster-sized collage displays into which you put other quotes from the play as word bubbles, characters' names, your own ideas, pictures and headlines from newspapers and magazines and your own illustrations. Here are suggestions for what to include in a poster, for the oxymoron 'loving hate'.

LOVING	L	HATE
words	O	words
quotations } *from play and elsewhere*	V	quotations } *from play and elsewhere*
pictures	I	pictures
showing	N	*showing*
peaceful scenes	G	fighting
caring	H	war
loving	A	brawling
parents and children	T	people with hateful
Nurse and Juliet	E	expressions

Imagery: poster

Much of the powerful impact and atmosphere of foreboding in the play is made by the images which recur throughout the words spoken by most of the characters. You will have noticed several examples of recurring images as you worked on the play. Divide the class into six groups. Each group is going to produce an image poster for one of the sets of images listed below. Your poster should include about ten appropriate quotations from the play, each linked to your set of images, and a visual representation made up of your own drawings, or pictures taken from magazines or other sources. Your finished poster can be displayed in class for other groups to see. The class can then discuss as a whole what effect you think these images have on your feelings about the events of the play, and the impressions you are left with at the end.

The images to work on are:

- night – moon, stars, dark, sky
- day – sun, daylight, dawn
- light – brightness, lantern, torch, meteor, shine
- eyes – sight, eyes, look, seem, appear, weep, tears
- beauty – fair, bright, desire
- death – Death, mourn, grave, monument, tomb, corpse, funeral

An image for the play – poster or book cover

You can extend your work on the play's imagery by deciding with a partner on one or two central images which you feel sum up what the play is about. Use your idea as the main illustration on a poster advertising a performance of the play, or as a cover for a new edition of the text. Add appropriate titles and words to your illustration.

Names

Romeo is a Montague, Juliet is a Capulet. Their names, particularly Romeo's name, come to have a significance far beyond their function simply as names. For Juliet, the name 'Montague' means enemy, for Romeo the name 'Capulet' means foe.

Produce with a partner a Montague and a Capulet list of all the references in the play to these names, and any other references to names (for example, when Juliet says, 'Tis but thy name that is my enemy'). Add in the names of the speakers, and then discuss and note down your answers to these questions:

■ Is one name mentioned more than the other?
■ Is a name seen as something you can get rid of?
■ What reaction is sparked off in Capulets when the name 'Montague' is mentioned?
■ What reaction is sparked off in Montagues when the name 'Capulet' is mentioned?
■ Can you think of modern examples of names producing violent responses?
■ What conclusions do you come to about the importance of names?

Time

Each scene introduction has helped you keep track of the time in the play as it moves so quickly from Sunday morning to Thursday morning. The references to time of day and day of the week are pointed and deliberate. The audience is being given a clear and inescapable sense of how time is passing.

You may also have noticed that different impressions are given about time by the way characters talk about it for other reasons.

The *past* is frequently talked about, the *present* seems to be much more drawn out than just four or five days, and the *future* is predicted and hoped for. The following work focuses your attention on the past and the future.

Divide the class into two groups, each group to work on one of these two aspects of time. Within your groups, you can divide up the play so that more than one person works on each act.

Copy the appropriate chart on page 95 onto a large sheet of paper. Fill in your group's findings, with short quotes from the play. The charts can then be displayed and compared by the class. Discuss how this talking about time affects your ideas about the play.

Count as the past anything which happened before the play starts. Count as the future anything which is talked about as happening 'in time to come', **after** the play is over.

Chart for the past

Speaker and reference	What event is talked about	When in the past happened
Prince Act 1 scene 1	'Three civil brawls'	We don't know
Prince	Feud started 'bred of an airy word'	A long time ago

Chart for the future

Speaker and reference	What is talked about
Prince Act 1 scene 1	Future brawls, threat of death as punishment 'If ever you disturb our streets again'
Capulet Act 1 scene 2	Juliet marrying Paris in two years' time. 'Let two more summers wither in their pride'

Type of play

Romeo and Juliet was written in about 1595 and is Shakespeare's second tragedy. In very simple terms, a tragedy is a play in which the leading character or characters die by the end. In Shakespeare's tragedies the ending also seems to bring a particular way of living to an end, too. It is quite hard to see what future there is for the Montagues and the Capulets after the deaths of Romeo and Juliet. As powerful families in Verona, they have no one to pass on their wealth and position to. At the end they can only talk about using their wealth to put up golden statues to their two dead children.

In tragedy, there is always a sense that 'if only' certain things hadn't happened, everything would have turned out all right. This is quite strongly conveyed in *Romeo and Juliet*, through several key incidents which turn the course of events towards the deaths of the five young people.

If only

Divide the class into twelve groups, each group to look at two scenes. In your scenes, look for events which could be called 'if only' events – if they hadn't happened, the play would have been different.

Find as many as you can, list them with details of who was involved in them, and what happened as a result. Then come together as a class, and present your lists in turn, saying the words 'if only' before each of your statements. For example:

Act 1 scene 1: 'If only Sampson and Gregory had not provoked a street fight that morning, the Prince would not have threatened death if it happened again.'

Act 1 scene 1: 'If only Romeo hadn't been so miserably in love, he wouldn't have irritated Benvolio and they wouldn't have gone to the Capulets' feast.'

Act 3 scene 5: 'If only the Nurse had helped Juliet, Juliet wouldn't have gone to Friar Laurence and taken the potion.'

What would happen to the play if any of the 'if only' statements were to come true? Discuss your responses to these ideas as a class.